Make Your Own Cosmetics!

Volume 1

Recipes for
Color Cosmetics

Karin Bombeli
&
Thomas Bombeli, M.D.

First Edition

SOMERSET
Cosmetic Company, LLC

Make Your Own Cosmetics!
Volume I
Recipes for Color Cosmetics
By
Karin Bombeli & Thomas Bombeli, M.D.

First Edition
Copyright © 2007 by Somerset Cosmetic Company, LLC
All rights reserved
ISBN: 0-9658528-4-9

Photographs & Layout by:
Somerset Cosmetic Company, LLC

Published by:
Somerset Cosmetic Company, LLC
P. O. Box 3372, Renton, WA 98059
Email: somerset@makingcosmetics.com
Website: www.makingcosmetics.com

Printed & bound in Hong Kong

About the Authors

Karin and Thomas Bombeli are married and grew up in Zurich, Switzerland. They later moved to the United States, and have lived there for several years. For more than 15 years, Karin has nurtured a keen interest in the manufacture of cosmetics and toiletries. Mainly through self-education, Karin continuously extended her knowledge about cosmetic chemistry. Soon she established a cosmetic laboratory and started producing her own cosmetic products. After graduating several college courses regarding the production and technology of cosmetics and toiletries, her hobby finally became her profession. In 1997, Karin founded Somerset Cosmetic Company, which was one of the first companies in the United States to specialize in handcrafted cosmetics. The company has rapidly established itself as the leading source of cosmetic ingredients and recipes for all individuals and companies producing their own cosmetics on a small scale.

Karin is author of the book *Modern & Healthy Body Care,* which was published in 1997. It was the first book that not only described food-based kitchen cosmetics, but also provided methods and recipes that allowed everybody to make truly professional skin and hair care products. In 2002, Karin published a second book titled *Recipes for Makeup Products,* which described how to make your own lipsticks, mascara, eyeliners, foundations and mineral makeup. Both books have met with an enthusiastic response and have sold thousands of copies.

Thomas is a medical doctor who graduated from Medical School at the University of Bern, Switzerland, in 1987. He further specialized in internal medicine and laboratory medicine. Based on his experience of more than 12 years in medical research laboratories, Thomas brought much technical knowledge and expertise to Karin's cosmetic laboratory. Inspired from the many discussions with Karin on how to develop and improve cosmetic formulations, Thomas became increasingly interested and involved in cosmetic chemistry. In addition, with the background as medical doctor, Thomas always took great care about using cosmetic ingredients that are truly effective and do not harm skin and hair.

Thomas is author of more than 30 scientific articles published in various international, peer-reviewed medical journals. He also published a book about laboratory medicine. Thomas now works primarily for Somerset Cosmetic Company, and continues to work as a medical and laboratory consultant.

Table of Contents

Introduction

About this Book

This book is essentially a new edition of the book *Recipes for Makeup Products,* which was first published in 2002. The book has received such an enthusiastic response that we had to reprint it three times within the last four years. Despite this success, however, we decided to give the book a complete overhaul. We gave the book a new title, a completely new design and layout, more recipes, additional how-to-do picture series, more detailed descriptions of cosmetic ingredients, and, last but not least, an index.

For those who already have the previous book *Recipes for Makeup Products*, this book will now provide you with more detailed information on how to manufacture great color cosmetics. For example, the manufacturing procedures are now depicted in a new, more informative step-by-step picture series, and more detailed descriptions. In addition, all cosmetic ingredients used for the recipes are now described in much more detail to give you more information about why and how a particular ingredient is used. Besides additional recipes, you will see that previous recipes may have been changed a bit in order to introduce new ingredients, or simply to improve the quality or performance of the product. You may, however, still find recipes that remained unchanged. We have also added some more complex formulas with more ingredients and more steps in the procedure, as many of the readers of the previous book have become experienced cosmetics-makers.

For those readers who are new to this hobby, this book will demystify the world of cosmetics manufacturing. You will see that making your own lipstick, eyeliner, or mineral makeup is not a mystery, but as simple as mixing food ingredients for a cake. You will also learn many new ingredients that you possibly have never heard of before (this may also help you to understand the labels of commercial products).

Even though all recipes give ready-to-use products, we encourage you to modify recipes to your own needs. Don't be afraid of trying new formulas and experimenting with new ideas, this helps you to become a better cosmetics-maker! And don't forget: Have fun!

Making Your Own Cosmetics

Since the publication of our first book *Modern & Healthy Body Care* in 1997, we have received many enthusiastic letters from readers expressing their excitement about making their own personal care products. Many of the readers were astonished about the fact that it is even possible at all to manufacture cosmetics at home. We have also received responses from experienced cosmetics makers, who have been producing their own cosmetics for many years. Interestingly, their standards of quality are no longer retail products, but vice versa; their own handcrafted products have become the benchmark against which retail products are measured! Furthermore, we also know of readers who have started their own business selling their products very successfully.

Sure, the manufacture of cosmetics can also become a fastidious task requiring lots of expertise, special raw materials and equipment, like in the laboratories of large cosmetic companies. But let's keep it simple! The basic procedures are always the same. You don't need 20 to 30 ingredients to make a good lipstick, and you don't need to attend chemistry classes to understand how thickeners work, or what an emulsion is. It's all about trying, rather than theory.

Making your own cosmetics also does not mean that you have to completely abandon your favorite commercial products. Most people utilize their handcrafted products in addition to retail products. Sure, there are people who exclusively use their own products.

Reasons for doing so are the many advantages that homemade products have over commercial products:

• **To individualize products**: You can add the ingredients you really want such as botanicals, essential oils, fragrances or active ingredients, and omit the ones you don't like.

• **To make truly natural products**: Too often the label 'all-natural' on retail products does not hold what it promises, as the majority of the ingredients are still synthetic! Homemade products are really all-natural, as you can use exclusively pure organic and truly natural ingredients.

• **To make more effective products**: You can add active ingredients at concentrations that are really effective, not in trace amounts like many retail products do, just to be able to list the ingredients on the label.

• **To make non-irritant products**: Avoid the time-consuming and frustrating search for cosmetics that don't contain the ingredient(s) your skin doesn't tolerate well. By making your own products, you can easily omit all such irritants or other harsh chemicals.

Remember, the key word in making your own cosmetics is *"create"*! As mentioned before, don't be afraid to experiment with the recipes by adding your favorite botanicals, essential oils, fragrances, or active ingredients. Also, feel free to omit any ingredients you don't believe necessary to the formula, or to which you may have an allergy. For those of us who routinely suffer from skin allergies brought on by traditional, commercial cosmetics, this can provide a way to isolate problem ingredients that are often not a necessary component to the end product. Just be sure to read up on what the ingredient's role is before deciding to omit it from your recipe.

For the entrepreneurial spirit that is alive in so many of us these days, one other benefit of learning how to make cosmetics is the option to branch out and create a home based business in which your favorite creations are sold online and/or to local spas and salons. The demand for personalized products is continuing to grow each year and shows no sign of stopping. Gone are the days of "one size fits all" cosmetics. Today, women are more in tune with their bodies and their beauty needs and are looking for products that address the issues most pressing for their needs.

Mark our words: we believe that we haven't seen the end of the homemade cosmetics industry. In fact, we would be willing to bet that we have barely seen the beginning. With recipes that are both varied and complex enough to keep even the most voracious of beauty product appetites assuaged, and simple enough that even busy business women (or men) have no trouble finding the time to whip them up in a few spare minutes, this is a trend that is expanding into thousands of households and will undoubtedly spread to include a new industry of personalized products.

Handcrafted cosmetics are easy to make and have a professional appearance and performance

Equipment & Methods

The Right Equipment

You don't need to set up an entire chemistry laboratory for making your own cosmetics. Some tools, however, are essential and should be acquired. Things just go easier! There is some basic equipment that you will always need, and some special tools that are necessary only for some specific products.

recipe, objectives (type of final product and its properties), ingredients, concentration of ingredients (percentages, weights or volumes), procedure (including heating temperatures, stirring times etc.), results (what went well, what failed), and conclusions (what needs to be modified next time).

Basic Equipment

This includes two heat-resistant glass beakers, measuring cups and spoons, a scale, a laboratory thermometer, pH indicator paper, pipettes, spatulas, a hand mixer, and paper towel. The glass beakers are the actual "brewing pots" in which you add the ingredients to melt, mix and stir them into the final product. Make sure that the beakers are made of heat-resistant glass, as they need to be heated to up to 190°F (88°C). A hand mixer or milk-frothing mixer are ideal for stirring liquids such as emulsions or dispersions.

The pH indicator paper may be utilized more often for making toiletries rather than color cosmetics. There are, however, situations where you need to know how acidic or alkaline a cosmetic product is (e.g. foundation creams).

Last but not least, you should keep a lab notebook. A notebook is as important a tool as all the other tools mentioned above. It allows you to record methods and formulas, repeat experiments, retrieve information and document new ideas. Each time when making a recipe, you should include the following information in your notebook: date, source of

Basic Equipment
- 2 heat resistant glass beakers (e.g. 250 ml and 400 ml)
- Scale, measuring cups/spoons
- Laboratory thermometer
- pH indicator paper
- Hand mixer or milk frother
- Pipettes & spatulas
- Paper towel
- Notebook

Although this list may look very long and exhaustive, it is really worthwhile to go the extra mile. Imagine: you want to reproduce a great lipstick recipe but had not (or only incompletely) written down what equipment, ingredients and procedure you had originally used! Making good use of your notebook makes things so much easier on yourself.

Special Equipment

Some special tools are needed for making specific cosmetic products. In particular, a mortar and pestle will be necessary if you need to blend pigments or disperse pigments in oils (called wetting). Pigments, particularly iron oxide pigments, consist of grainy particles that have a strong tendency to stick to each other, forming aggregates and clumps.

So, they need to be grinded down to break the aggregates in order to ensure that the particles are in fine form. This milling process is the only one that ensures that the powder has uniform and homogenous color. We do not recommend the use of wooden mortars, since they are difficult to disinfect, and tend to absorb oils and colors over time. Mortars made of plastic, metal or clay are acceptable. If you plan to blend or wet larger quantities of pigments, a mortar may not be the optimal tool. The filling capacity of mortars is rather small and the milling work with the pestle is hard and arduous. Instead, you may want to use a common kitchen food processor (e.g. Hamilton Beach) that is able to chop, mince, and mix. In our hands, it gave surprisingly good results.

A lipstick mold is the main tool for making color lipsticks, lip gloss sticks, and cover sticks. Molds, however, are difficult to obtain. We are not aware of any companies in the United States (except us) that sell lipstick molds that are suitable for the home use. The cosmetic industry utilizes large automatic or semi-automatic molding systems that cost tens of thousands of dollars. There are also some manually operated molds available for making smaller quantities of about 12 - 36 lipsticks. They are made of stainless steel and still cost several hundred dollars.

We have, therefore, designed and produced our own lipstick mold, specifically for small-scale home use. It is a three-cavity mold for making 3 lipsticks at the time. It is made of special, exceptionally solid, heat-resistant plastic, allowing you to use it unlimited times. Best of all, the mold costs less than 20 dollars.

For making eyeliners and lip liners, you will need hollow pencils and medical syringes. The syringes are used to fill the hot and liquid color solution into the pencils.

Special Equipment
- Mortar and pestle
- Syringe (e.g. 5 ml or 10 ml)
- Lipstick mold

Mortar and pestle are necessary to blend and wet pigments

Ideal "pots" for making cosmetics are heat-resistant glass beakers with scales

Re-usable 3-cavity lipstick mold (design by Somerset Cosmetic Co., LLC)

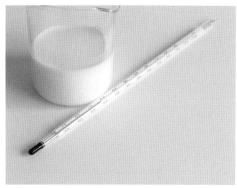

A laboratory thermometer is important to heat or cool mixtures very acurately

pH indicators are needed to measure the acidity or alkalinity of a formula

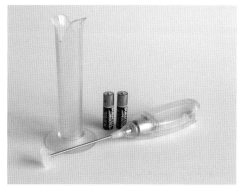

A milk frother is useful to mix low amounts of liquids or to dissolve powdery ingredients

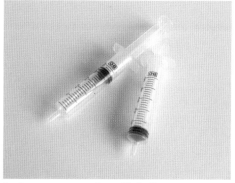

Syringes are used to fill hollow pencils for making eyeliners or lip liners

Basics About Mixing

The manufacture of cosmetics and toiletries involves the mixing of various solid and liquid raw materials with each other, often in the presence of heating and cooling. In the manufacture of color cosmetics, solid/solid mixing techniques are most frequent.

Solid/Solid Mixing

Most powders used for producing cosmetics are cohesive powders, which means that the individual particles tend to stick together forming small clumps. Pigments, both inorganic (iron oxides and ultramarines) and organic pigments (lakes and dyes), tend to aggregate. As mentioned above, it is necessary to break down aggregates in order to make powder mixtures homogenous, and in case of pigments, to fully develop their colors. Professional cosmetic laboratories use either ribbon blenders, which use a tossing motion to break clumps apart, or high-shear milling devices, which use hammers. For the small-scale production at home, the clumps can be crushed and grinded manually with a mortar and pestle (see previous page).

In order to facilitate the subsequent incorporation of powders into an aqueous or oily phase of a formula, often a small amount of liquid is added to the mortar during the milling process. This procedure is called wetting, or pre-dispersion (see below). As most pigments are water-insoluble, oil is usually utilized as a wetting liquid. This liquid, however, forms a film around the particles and, as a consequence, promotes the formation of clumps. Therefore, an even stronger mixing action must be applied. By adding a small amount of an emulsifier, such liquid-induced aggregate formation can be reduced. In most powder formulas, however, the presence of an emulsifier is not desirable.

Dispersions

Dispersions are mixtures of solid, insoluble particles (powders) and a liquid. Effective dispersions require the powder to be pre-wetted. Wetting is done by mixing a small amount of a liquid into the powder before it is added to the liquid phase of the formula.

Solid/Liquid Mixing

Mixing solid particles in a liquid solution is a frequent procedure in the manufacture of cosmetics. If the solid particles are soluble in the liquid (either oil or water), mixing is easy and can be done by a simple propeller stirrer, such as a kitchen mixer or milk-frothing mixer. A typical example is the dissolution of water-soluble dyes (e.g. D&C Red 33) in water. If the solid particles, however, are insoluble or only partially soluble, they can only be distributed, but not dissolved, in the liquid. Such a mixture is called dispersion.

Wetting is the process that greatly facilitates the preparation of dispersions. As mentioned above, by mixing a small amount of a liquid into solid ingredients (e.g. pigments, gums, talc), the solid particles get attached to liquid droplets—or in other words, they get pre-wetted or pre-dispersed. Effective wetting, however, requires that all the solid aggregates be broken down. If there are still clumps, the wetting process is incomplete, as the inner part of the clumps had not been in contact with the liquid. To obtain a homogenous and effective dispersion, the solid particles must be completely wetted out by the liquid.

To incorporate pre-wetted powders into a liquid, vigorous agitation is required. Professional laboratories use different types of sophisticated mixing and stirring devices with various flow patterns and turbulences. For the home use, a simple paddle stirrer, or kitchen hand mixer, works just fine. They produce enough turbulences and flow to create stable dispersions. In thick and viscous liquids the effectiveness may be limited, though. To avoid air entrapment, the mixer should be placed at the very bottom of the container.

Liquid/Liquid Mixing

No special equipment is necessary if all the liquids that need to be mixed are miscible. Stirring can be done with a spoon, a simple kitchen hand mixer, or a milk-frothing mixer. The droplets of the liquids mix and mingle with each other so that there is no boundary between the two liquids.

If the liquids are immiscible, however, the mixture will separate again, even after vigorous stirring. Water and oil are a typical example. When mixed together, they stay as two separate layers with a clear boundary between them. The reason is that the attraction forces of oil and water particles are very different. Oil particles are only weakly held together and cannot overcome the strong attraction forces between the water particles. Consequently, the oil drops cannot stay between water particles, but form a separate layer.

In order to mix oil and water, you have to make an emulsion. With the addition of an emulsifier, oil and water can be forced to mix. Emulsifiers are molecules consisting of a water-loving (hydrophilic) part and oil-loving (lipophilic) part. With their lipophilic part, emulsifiers wrap around and incorporate oil drops, preventing them from reuniting again and forming a separate layer. In this way, the oil particles are shielded from each other and spread throughout the water. Such single droplets form the dispersed phase, while the dispersion liquid is called the continuous phase. An emulsion can be defined as: a mixture made of an immiscible liquid dispersed in another liquid in the form of tiny droplets.

Emulsions
Emulsions are mixtures of two immiscible liquids like oil and water where one of the liquids is dispersed in the other liquid in the form of tiny droplets that are stabilized by an emulsifier.

If an oily liquid is dispersed in water the emulsion is called oil-in-water (o/w) emulsion; and vice versa, if water droplets are dispersed in oil, the resulting emulsion is called water-in-oil (w/o) emulsion. Typically, o/w-emulsions are chosen for applications requiring a relatively small amount of fatty material, like hand, shaving or moisturizing creams. On the other hand, w/o-emulsions are preferred when a larger amount of oil is desired. This system has a greasier feel and leaves a longer-lasting residue. Typical products are emollient creams and sunscreens.

Besides simple two-phase emulsion, there are also more complex, multiple-phase emulsions as w/o/w (w/o emulsion in water) or o/w/o emulsions (o/w emulsion in oil).

To stabilize emulsions, the mixture of oil, water and emulsifier must be stirred well. Cosmetic laboratories often mix emulsions in two phases. First, while the emulsifier is being added, the oil-water mixture is stirred with the rotor-stator mixer at relatively low speed. In the second phase, the emulsion is then passed through a high-shear mixer, such as a homogenizer. For the home-based cosmetics maker, emulsions can be stirred best with a hand mixer. For the manufacture of decorative cosmetics, emulsions are typically needed for the preparation of cream foundations

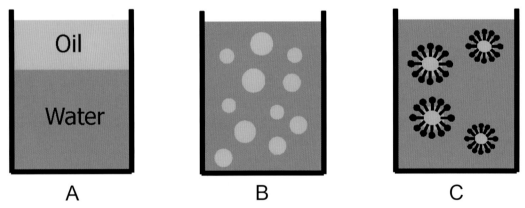

A

B

C

How Emulsifiers Work: Without agitation (figure A) oil floats on the water as a separate layer. After agitation (figure B) the oil is broken down to tiny droplets which are dispersed in the water. To avoid the oil droplets to be reunited to a single layer, an emulsifier is added (figure C) which wraps around the oil droplets and prevents them from being bound to each other. The emulsion is now stabilized.

Getting Prepared

A good preparation is essential to produce cosmetics better, easier, faster, and more successfully. Here is a checklist of what you should do before starting:

Familiarize yourself with the recipe: One of the most important preparatory steps is to read and understand the formula. Don't start mixing ingredients without knowing what the ingredient's properties and functions are, and how the formula is structured. If you have bought the ingredients at Somerset Cosmetic Company you can easily get all the information on the label including source, use, properties and applications. If you have obtained the ingredients somewhere else and don't have instructions how to use it, we strongly advise you to search for more information. Only when you know why a certain ingredient is added, you will fully understand how a product is manufactured, and how it may be modified or further improved.

Review the procedure: Another reason to carefully read the recipe before starting to mix is the fact that most recipes are composed of various phases, which need to be prepared separately in different containers and mixed together in a specific order. In addition, certain ingredients need to be pre-mixed (e.g. pigments usually need to be pre-wetted), before they can be introduced into a recipe.

Assemble all the ingredients: To avoid the painful and costly experience of throwing away an almost finished recipe just because one indispensable ingredient was missing, it is important to gather the necessary raw materials *before* beginning a batch.

Disinfect tools and containers: Avoid growth of bacteria and fungi. Microbes can not only damage your cosmetic product, but also induce skin infections. Therefore, always disinfect all containers and tools you use for making and storing your products. Isopropyl alcohol (rubbing alcohol) or 70% alcohol (ethyl alcohol) are both acceptable.

Prepare adequate packaging: Filling your product into a nice container is the final touch of your work. Don't be too focused on the design; practical aspects are also important. Thick and viscous products, for example, may dispense better in wide-mouth jars.

Label all your products: When your cosmetic product is completed, remember to attach a label that provides information about the type of product, date of production and perhaps also the ingredients used. The date is particularly important to monitor the shelf life. If you consider selling your products, please check the FDA labeling regulations in the FDA website (http://www.cfsan.fda.gov).

Safe Handling of Ingredients

Making cosmetics is not dangerous, but following some basic safety rules is important to ensure that the handling of raw materials will not do any harm to you or the environment, and to avoid having your products become skin irritants or allergenic.

Avoid harsh ingredients: The use of exclusively mild and non-irritant ingredients is one of the major benefits of handcrafted cosmetics. Take advantage of this! There are still various raw materials available on the market that have long been shown to be harsh and irritating to the skin. It may be time-consuming to check resources (see below) about their potential harshness.

Good suppliers, however, should provide you all the data necessary to determine whether a specific ingredient is truly mild, or possibly an irritant and/or allergenic.

Avoid poorly labeled ingredients: There are, unfortunately, still many suppliers offering cosmetic ingredients with very poor labeling! For example, active ingredients are often sold without any information about their activity, use level, concentration, and mode of action. Consider such ingredients to be impure, highly diluted and not of cosmetic or pharmaceutical grade quality.

Sometimes, ingredients are offered with only a trade name but no generic or chemical name. So, you don't know what you are actually using. In such cases ask the supplier for the INCI name (International Nomenclature of Cosmetic Ingredients), the MSDS (Material Safety Data Sheet), and possibly the COA (Certificate of Analysis) of the product. Only with this information will you know the kind of substance with which you are dealing. It speaks for itself that you should no longer buy ingredients from suppliers whom you have to ask for these documents each time, or who may not even be able to provide you these documents.

Avoid unsafe ingredients: By US law, FDA does not have the authority to approve cosmetic products or ingredients, except for colors. There are only a few ingredients that are prohibited by the FDA. To ensure safety of cosmetic ingredients, the cosmetic industry, in combination with government, has undertaken a program to establish lists of ingredients that are safe to use in cosmetics. The regulations identify cosmetic ingredients as either safe, unsafe, or undecided when further information is required.

Unfortunately, there are many websites publishing lists of "unsafe cosmetic ingredients" based on no scientific evidence, thereby discrediting many good and completely safe ingredients. True and validated scientific evidence about the safety of cosmetic ingredients can be found only at these resources:

• CIR Reports (Cosmetic Ingredient Review): US organization consisting of toxicologists, dermatologists, and members from the FDA, CTFA, and Consumer Federation of America.

• EEC Cosmetic Directives (European Union): Series of rules, principles, and lists of safe and unsafe ingredients.

• FDA Monographs: In the USA sunscreens, antiperspirants and skin protectants are treated as OTC (over the counter) "drugs" which are reviewed by experts to define the safety of them.

• IFRA (International Fragrance Association): Advisory committee of the manufacturers of fragrances issues recommendations about the safety of various fragrances.

• JACT reports (Journal of the American College of Toxicology): Publishes studies about the safety of cosmetic substances.

Avoid overheating ingredients: Be careful when heating oils, since they are flammable at certain temperatures. Spilling can produce severe burns, and when heated too long or at too high temperatures, many ingredients lose their activity and will no longer be effective. In general, active ingredients do not like to be heated, and should therefore be added only after the mixture has cooled down.

Avoid overdosing ingredients: While commercial cosmetic manufacturers may add active ingredients at too low a concentration, home-based producers often overcompensate and tend to use ingredients at too high a level. With most ingredients, this does no harm. There are, however, ingredients that can induce skin irritations when added at higher-than-recommended concentrations, including surfactants, fragrances, essential oils, skin lighteners, and preservatives.

Check safety data of ingredients: The vast majority of cosmetic ingredients are completely harmless when incorporated into a finished product. When handling ingredients in concentrated form, however, they may do harm, whether they are synthetic or natural. For example, inhalation of the dust of fine powders like pigments or sunscreens may irritate the respiratory tract, or contact of the eyes with undiluted surfactants, conditioners, or fragrances may lead to irritation of the eyes. When handling ingredients of which you don't know about their potential hazards, check the MSDS (Material Safety Data Sheet), which should be provided by the supplier.

It is always wise to wear disposable gloves and a mask when handling with fine powders or volatile liquids.

Strive for Good Quality

Even if you never intend to sell your cosmetic products, you should always aim to make products of the highest possible quality. Products of poor quality will make you rapidly lose your joy and interest in handcrafting cosmetics. Assuring consistent quality of your products involves several aspects:

Select only high-quality ingredients: As mentioned before, avoid buying ingredients that come without essential information like source, composition, purity and how to use it. Offered at cheap prices, such ingredients are often impure, ineffective and of very low quality. Typical examples include spoiled natural oils, inactive vitamins, poorly coloring non- cosmetic-grade pigments, diluted fragrances with poor (or no) scent, and ineffective active ingredients in non-preserved aqueous solutions that are contaminated with bacteria.

Store ingredients properly: Most raw materials have a long shelf life (months and years) when stored correctly. Whatever type of ingredient, always use a tightly closed container, and avoid moisture and extreme temperatures, as these conditions accelerate spoiling. Certain ingredients (e.g. vitamin C and E) should be stored light-protected, while others should be placed in the refrigerator (e.g. butters, active ingredients, vitamin A).

Use preservatives: Contamination with bacteria is a frequent problem of homemade cosmetics. Many people think that truly all-natural products do not contain preservatives. Non-preserved cosmetic products, however, typically have a shelf life of a few days, or perhaps 2 - 3 weeks when refrigerated. Thereafter, the products will contain massive amounts of bacteria and/or fungi, even if you don't see them. Understandably, applying such spoiled products is not desirable.

There are both natural and synthetic agents that inhibit the growth of bacteria and/or fungi. In general, natural preservatives including grapefruit seed or rosemary extract, potassium sorbate, sorbic acid, essential oils, and vitamin C and E are less effective than synthetic ones. However, based on their potent antioxidant activity vitamin C and E are still very important ingredients since they help prevent oils and fats from becoming rancid. Other widely used antioxidants and stabilizers are BHT (butylated hydroxy toluene) and EDTA.

Synthetic preservatives that are most often used include methylparaben, propylparaben, diazolidinyl urea, phenoxyethanol, DMDM hydantoin, benzyl alcohol, formaldehyde and triclosan. We recommend using phenoxyethanol combined with sorbic acid, or methyl/propylparaben combined with diazolidinyl urea because they are very effective but still very mild if used correctly. Thiomersal, quaterniumm-15 and formaldehyde have often been found to cause skin reactions.

Avoid extreme acidity and alkalinity: If formulas give poor results even though all manufacturing steps seemed to be performed correctly, it is often a problem of the pH value. Extreme acidity and alkalinity can result in poor product performance, or even skin irritation. The optimal pH range for cosmetics and personal care products is between 5 and 7. We recommend using a pH indicator (e.g. paper strips) to determine the pH value of your cosmetic product. When a product becomes too acidic (pH too low) or too alkaline (pH too high), you can easily correct the pH value by adding small amounts of triethanolamine or citric acid, respectively.

Control your finished product: when controlling your finished product, be critical with yourself. Check the consistency, color, scent, and where applicable, the spreadability, skin feel, and coverage. Whether you are happy with your product or not, write the results down into your notebook. If you think your product may be improved further, try to draw conclusions why it is a little too greasy, too thick, too thin, not homogenous, or doesn't have the exact shade you wanted. This helps you to modify your formulas and start experimenting. It is also a good starting point for creating your very own formulas.

Cosmetic ingredients of high quality and purity are prerequisites for producing good cosmetics.

Ingredients

Registries of Cosmetic Ingredients

The cosmetic industry uses its own terminology of cosmetic ingredients, which is different from any other chemical or biochemical nomenclature system. Originally established in the early 1970's by the CTFA (Cosmetic, Toiletry, and Fragrance Association), the cosmetic dictionary is the **INCI system** (International Nomenclature of Cosmetic Ingredients). Currently, the inventory of INCI-registered ingredients comprises more than 12,000 names and the list is continuously growing. Many countries, including the United States (but not Canada), Australia, Japan and the members of the European Union, require manufacturers of cosmetic ingredients to submit all new ingredients for registration in the INCI system.

Why should you care about the INCI system? First, if you are accustomed to the traditional IUPAC terminology of chemicals as it is taught in school, you will have difficulties identifying ingredients, as they may have completely different names (e.g. hexadecanol in IUPAC is cetyl alcohol in INCI). Second, if you make homemade cosmetic products to sell, for legal labeling requirements, you need to know the official INCI name for your ingredients. The complete INCI list can be obtained in CD-ROM or book format at the CTFA's website. A partial INCI list of about 6,000 entries is available for free at our website at www.makingcosmetics.com.

Another system that identifies ingredients is the **CAS system** (Chemical Abstract Service), which uses numbers. CAS registry numbers are unique numerical identifiers for chemical compounds. CAS, which is a division of the American Chemical Society, assigns these numbers to every chemical that has been described in the literature. CAS also maintains and sells a database of these chemicals, known as the CAS registry. About 23 million compounds have received a CAS number so far, with about 4,000 new ones being added each day. Almost all molecule databases today allow searching by CAS number.

If you want to sell your products, the ingredients on the label must wear the official INCI name

Although the CAS system is used internationally, there is another system in Europe called **EINECS** (European Inventory of Existing Commercial Chemical Substances). This system also uses numbers to identify chemicals, but its relatively limited scope of only about 100,000 chemicals makes it far less useful than the CAS system.

As mentioned before, when purchasing cosmetic ingredients you should not have to search by yourself for the INCI name, CAS or EINECS number. A good supplier provides this information to its customers without being asked for it.

Pigments & Dyes

Colors are divided into two categories: dyes and pigments. Dyes are colors that are soluble in the medium in which they are used (with some exceptions), whereas pigments are insoluble. Both dyes and pigments can be synthetic or natural. The majority of colors used in toiletries (such as shampoos, shower gels, creams, and lotions) are dyes, while pigments are more often used in color cosmetics.

Dyes & Organic Pigments

Dyes are generally water-soluble, although some are water-soluble only during application, after which they become insoluble. Additionally, some dyes are not water-soluble at all. Dyes are made of organic materials. Originally, dyes were obtained from plants such as indigo and madder, or from the shells of mollusks; today most dyes are made synthetically from coal tar and petrochemicals. As the chemical structure of dyes is relatively easy to modify, many new dyes are being synthesized. There are seven different chemical groups of dyes.

*   Indigoid (e.g. D&C Red 30)
*   Xanthene (e.g. D&C Yellow 7 & 8)
*   Azo (e.g. D&C Red 17 & 36)
*   Nitro (e.g. Ext. D&C Yellow 7)
*   Triphenylmethane (e.g. FD&C Blue 1)
*   Quinoline (e.g. D&C Yellow 10 & 11)
*   Anthraquinone (e.g. D&C Green 6)

Dyes can also be modified to become water-insoluble. Such insoluble dyes are called organic pigments. There are three classes:

Lakes: Lakes consist of an organic dye with an inorganic, usually metallic substrate (e.g. aluminum hydrate, aluminum benzoate, talc, zinc oxide or titanium dioxide). Lakes are typically used in products that do not have enough moisture to absorb the dye. Examples include oil-based products.

Toners: Toners are pigments that are made by precipitating a water-soluble dye as a metal salt like calcium, barium or stontium. Toners are also water-insoluble.

True Pigments: True pigments are not a modified dye, but colors that are water-insoluble based on their chemical structure.

Inorganic Pigments

Inorganic pigments are composed of insoluble metallic compounds (minerals) found in the earth. Inorganic pigments are, therefore, also called mineral pigments. By definition, inorganic pigments are water-insoluble. They are either chemically synthesized or derived from natural sources (e.g. china clay, carbon deposits). Inorganic colors do not have the same kinds of health risks as organic colors and, therefore, do not require certification (see further). On the other hand, inorganic pigments are not available in the range of shades that the organic colors offer. Inorganic pigments are oxides, silicates, or phosphates derived of such typical minerals as iron, manganese, chromium, aluminum, and titanium.

Iron Oxides: Iron oxides are non-toxic, naturally occurring inorganic pigments from iron (e.g. hematite, magnetite). They are usually a combination of ferrous or ferric oxides and other pigments such as manganese. Typical colors include black, red and brown, but many more shades can be produced synthetically. Iron oxides are insoluble but miscible in water and oils. They can be tinted with titanium dioxide to create lighter shades.

Ultramarines: Ultramarines are inorganic pigments consisting essentially of a silicate of aluminium and sodium with some sulfides or sulfates. In nature they occur as a proximate component of lapis lazuli. While the typical color is blue there are also various other shades available. Ultramarines are insoluble but miscible in water and oils. In the USA ultramarines are not allowed to be used in lipsticks.

Micas

Micas are the most important and the most fun colors to work with. Their color ranges way beyond the rainbow, and mixing creates even more unique and beautiful shades. Micas come in different particle sizes. The ones that are smaller than 20 microns give a satiny appearance while large micas with up to 150 microns provide a sparkle effect.

Muscovite is the most common mica mineral and is found in igneous rocks such as granites and granitic pegmatites as well as methamorphic rocks such as schists. Mica can be easily identified by the thin, transparent sheets that it cleaves into. Untreated micas are transparent and are thus coated with iron ox-

ide pigments (black, red, yellow) and titanium dioxide to create silver-white but also gold, copper and bronze shades. Others are coated with an additional layer of colored pigment including carmine, ferric ferrocyanide, D&C reds, chromium or aluminum oxide. This combination results in a brilliant color effect.

In addition, there are special effect micas called interference pigments which are coated only with titanium dioxide. These are minerals that cause polarized light to be split into two rays resulting micas to appear in different colors depending on the angle of view. This optical effect is caused by light interference. The different colors are achieved by controlling the thickness of the titanium dioxide layer and may be any hue in the spectrum.

Micas are usually added as a second color to achieve different shades and to add shimmer, but can also be used as the only color in a product if intense coloring is not desired, (e.g low color lipstick, lipgloss, blushes).

Solubility

Ideally, colorants used in cosmetics should not react with other ingredients in the formula. In addition, they should be stable during the manufacturing process and resistant towards changes of the temperature, pH value, and viscosity of the formula. As not all certified colors meet these requirements, only a small number of the colorants are used on a regular basis in the formulation of cosmetics.

The table below shows the solvents in which certified colors dissolve to give stable solutions. It must be emphasized, however, that colors that are insoluble in water, oils or liquid waxes can still be added to and mixed with these liquids! Although they won't go in solution, insoluble colors are easily miscible in water and oils and form a dispersion. For example, the insoluble lakes are often used in lipsticks and blushers.

Name	Water	Mineral Oil/Wax
FD&C Green No. 3	soluble	insoluble
FD&C Yellow No. 5	soluble	sol. in emulsions
FD&C Yellow No. 6	soluble	insoluble
FD&C Red No. 4	soluble	sol. in emulsions
FD&C Red No. 40	soluble	insoluble
FD&C Blue No. 1	soluble	mainly insoluble
D&C Green No. 5	soluble	sol. in emulsions
D&C Green No. 6	insoluble	moderately soluble
D&C Green No. 8	soluble	insoluble
D&C Yellow No. 7	insoluble	mainly insoluble
D&C Yellow No. 8	soluble	sol. in emulsions
D&C Yellow No. 10	soluble	insoluble
D&C Yellow No. 11	insoluble	soluble
D&C Red No. 6	soluble	insoluble
D&C Red No. 7	insoluble	mainly insoluble
D&C Red No. 17	insoluble	soluble
D&C Red No. 21	soluble	mainly insoluble
D&C Red No. 22	soluble	sol. in emulsions
D&C Red No. 27	insoluble	mainly insoluble
D&C Red No. 28	soluble	sol. in emulsions
D&C Red No. 30	insoluble	mainly insoluble
D&C Red No. 31	soluble	insoluble
D&C Red No. 33	soluble	insoluble
D&C Red No. 34	insoluble	mainly insoluble
D&C Red No. 36	insoluble	mainly insoluble
D&C Orange No. 4	soluble	sol. in emulsions
D&C Orange No. 5	insoluble	mainly insoluble
D&C Blue No. 4	soluble	mainly insoluble
D&C Brown No. 1	soluble	sol. in emulsions
D&C Violet No. 2	insoluble	soluble
Ext D&C Violet No. 2	soluble	insoluble
Ext D&C Yellow No. 7	soluble	insoluble

Use of Colors

Color Selection: when using dyes, you can choose between lakes and true dyes. Lakes are not soluble and may thus be preferred in dry color cosmetics. Lakes are also less likely to leave color stains on the skin, which is called bleeding. Dyes are soluble and may therefore be preferred in liquid makeup products and also to achieve long lasting color coverage, as in semi-permanent lipsticks. In general, dyes and lakes are used only in small amounts. For example, only about 1-3% of a red dye or lake is necessary to give a lipstick a red color.

Main Color and Shade: Typically, colors are mixed using one to three main colors, and one to three shading colors. The main colors make up the largest percentage of all the colorants and give a deep, rich tone (masstone). The shading colors are added at smaller amounts and give the masstone a certain shade. For example, to make a red lipstick with a slight yellow shade, the main part of the color mixture may consist of D&C Red No. 6 Ba Lake and D&C Red No. 7 Ca Lake, and only a small amount of FD&C yellow 5 Al Lake would be added. Typical shading colors are micas which give also a nice gloss.

Oil Absorption: Many colors have the tendency to absorb oil from the formula, thereby causing 'oil deficiency' in a product. This problem is mainly seen with organic colors, particularly aluminum lakes, rather than inorganic colors like iron oxides. Oil deficiency plays a role primarily in lipsticks where it may reduce the hardness of the stick.

Typical Use of Inorganic Colors

Name	Lipsticks	Face Makeup	Eye Makeup
Iron Oxide Black	some use	major use	major use
Iron Oxide Red	some use	some use	major use
Iron Oxide Orange	some use	major use	major use
Iron Oxide Yellow	some use	major use	major use
Iron Oxide Brown	some use	major use	major use
Chrom. Oxide Green	prohibited in US	not recommended	major use
Ultramarine Blue	prohibited in US	some use	major use
Ultramarine Pink	prohibited in US	some use	major use
Ultramarine Violet	prohibited in US	some use	major use
Manganese Violet	some use	not recommended	major use
Ferric Ferrocyanide	prohibited in US	not recommended	major use

Regulation

Colorants are the most highly regulated chemicals used in cosmetic products. All other cosmetic ingredients, except preservatives and certain active ingredients, do not need the approval of a regulatory authority. Currently, the FDA has approved 64 colorants for cosmetic use which are divided into two groups such as certifiable colors and exempt colors.

Certifiable Colors: These colors are defined as synthetic, organic colorants and must be batch certified. This means that the manufacturer of the color must submit each batch of color to the FDA for analysis and approval. Colorants that are approved for cosmetic use are designated either as FD&C (certified for use in food, drugs and cosmetics), D&C (certified for use in drugs and cosmetics including those in contact with mucous membranes and those that are ingested), or External D&C (certified for use in drugs and cosmetics that do not come in contact with mucous membranes or those that are ingested).

Exempt Colors: These colors are defined as the non-synthetic organic colors and inorganic colors. Batch certification is not required. Both certifiable and exempt colors are also subject to restriction rules in terms of their application and quantity. The use restriction dictates whether a colorant can be used in any cosmetic product, or must be restricted to products that are only externally applied and do not come in contact with mucous membranes. The quantity restriction dictates how much of a particular color may be used in a cosmetic product. Typically, such restrictions are in the range from 0.01% to 5%. For most colors, however, there is no clearly defined quantity restriction.

It is notable that the regulations vary from region to region. For example, micas, which are on the approval list of the FDA, are not considered a colorant in Europe and Japan. Further, ferric ferrocyanide may be used only in externally applied cosmetics in the US, while the EU and Japan also allow for lip area use. It is therefore wise to check the region's regulations for each colorant before use.

Permitted Certifiable Colors

Name	Use Restrictions in USA	Quantity Restrictions in USA
FD&C Green No. 3	Not for use in eye area	Consistent with GMP
FD&C Yellow No. 5	none	Consistent with GMP
FD&C Yellow No. 6	Not for use in eye area	Consistent with GMP
FD&C Red No. 4	External only	Consistent with GMP
FD&C Red No. 40	None	Consistent with GMP
FD&C Blue No. 1	None	Consistent with GMP
D&C Green No. 5	None	Consistent with GMP
D&C Green No. 6	Not for use in eye area	Consistent with GMP
D&C Green No. 8	Not for use in eye area	0.01% by weight
D&C Yellow No. 7	External only	Consistent with GMP
D&C Yellow No. 8	External only	Consistent with GMP
D&C Yellow No. 10	Not for use in eye area	Consistent with GMP
D&C Yellow No. 11	External only	Consistent with GMP
D&C Red No. 6	Not for use in eye area	Consistent with GMP
D&C Red No. 7	Not for use in eye area	Consistent with GMP
D&C Red No. 17	External only	Consistent with GMP
D&C Red No. 21	Not for use in eye area	Consistent with GMP
D&C Red No. 22	Not for use in eye area	Consistent with GMP
D&C Red No. 27	Not for use in eye area	Consistent with GMP
D&C Red No. 28	Not for use in eye area	Consistent with GMP
D&C Red No. 30	Not for use in eye area	Consistent with GMP
D&C Red No. 31	External only	Consistent with GMP
D&C Red No. 33	Not for use in eye area	3.0% in lipstick
D&C Red No. 34	External only	Consistent with GMP
D&C Red No. 36	Not for use in eye area	3.0% in lipstick
D&C Orange No. 4	External only	Consistent with GMP
D&C Orange No. 5	Not for use in eye area	5.0% un lipstick
D&C Orange No. 10	External only	Consistent with GMP
D&C Orange No. 11	External only	Consistent with GMP
D&C Blue No. 4	External only	Consistent with GMP
D&C Brown No. 1	External only	Consistent with GMP
D&C Violet No. 2	External only	Consistent with GMP
Ext D&C Violet No. 2	External only	Consistent with GMP
Ext D&C Yellow No. 7	External only	Consistent with GMP

*External means that the color must not come in contact with mucous membranes
**Color may be safely used in amounts consistent with good manufacturing practice
(GMP is an international quality assurance standard)

Permitted Exempt Colors

Name	Permitted Uses			
	Ingested	**External**	**Eye Area**	**Comment**
Aluminum Powder	No	Yes	Yes	
Annato	Yes	Yes	Yes	
Bismuth Citrate	No	Yes	Yes	0.5% in hair color
Bismuth Oxychloride	Yes	Yes	Yes	
Bronze Powder	Yes	Yes	Yes	
Carmel	Yes	Yes	Yes	
Carmine	Yes	Yes	Yes	
Carotene	Yes	Yes	Yes	
Chlorophyll-Cu Complex	Yes	No	No	For dentifrices only, at 0.1% max.
Chromium Hydroxide Green	No	Yes	Yes	
Chromium Oxide Green	No	Yes	Yes	
Copper Powder	Yes	Yes	Yes	
Dihydroxy Acetone	No	Yes	No	
Disodium EDTA Copper	No	Yes	No	
Ferric Ammonium Ferrocyanide	No	Yes	Yes	
Ferric Ferrocyanide	No	Yes	Yes	
Guaizulene	No	Yes	No	
Henna	No	Yes	No	For use in hair only
Iron Oxides	Yes	Yes	Yes	
Lead Acetate	No	Yes	No	
Manganese Violet	Yes	Yes	Yes	
Mica	Yes	Yes	Yes	
Pyrophyllite	No	Yes	No	
Silver	No	Yes	No	For nail polish only, at 1% max.
Titanium Dioxide	Yes	Yes	Yes	
Ultramarines	No	Yes	Yes	
Zinc Oxide	Yes	Yes	Yes	

Glossary of Ingredients

Allantoin **Description**: 5-ureidohydantoin. CAS# 97-59-6. Natural active ingredient derived from roots & leaves of the comfrey plant. Melting point 230°C (446°F). White crystalline powder, odorless. Water soluble (1g/200ml). **Properties**: protects skin, repairing agent promoting keratolysis & cell proliferation, relieves dryness, soothing effects. **Use**: add to water phase, use level 0.2 - 2%.

Almond Oil **Description**: amygdalae oleum dulcium. CAS# 8007-69-0. Natural oil pressed from the seeds of the sweet almond tree, contains 62-86% oleic acid, 20-30% linoleic acid & other valuable fatty acids, rich in beta-sitosterol, squalene & vitamin E. Insoluble in water. Pale yellow liquid, nutty odor. **Properties**: excellent emollient & moisturizer, good nourishing & revitalizing effect (penetrates the skin), heals chapped skin. **Use**: can be used as is, use level 1-100%.

Aloe Vera **Description**: natural gel derived from the interior of the leaves of the Aloe plant (aloe barbadensis Miller), consists of amino acids, enzymes, hormones, minerals, saponins, sterols, starch, lectins & vitamins, pH: 3.5-4.7. Water-soluble. CAS# 8001-97-6. Clear liquid, faint herbal odor. **Properties**: potent moisturizer, regenerating & healing agent, anti-inflammatory & anti-aging effects (increases collagen synthesis). **Use**: use as is, use level 1-100%.

Argireline **Description**: peptide (acetyl hexa-peptide-3) that inhibits the release of adrenalin & noradrenalin in neuronal skin cells blocking facial skin muscle tightening, a mechanism responsible for wrinkle formation. CAS# 616204-22-9. Contains 0.05% argireline in water. Clear liquid, odorless. Water soluble. **Properties**: relaxes facial tension leading to a reduction in superficial facial lines & wrinkles with regular use. **Use**: add to water phase, use level 5%.

Avocado Butter **Descriptions**: Persea Gratissima (avocado) seed oil. CAS# 91770-40-0. Natural seed oil from the flesh of the avocado fruit. Hydrogenated with soybean lipids and beeswax to a creamy texture. Soft, creamy butter, no odor. Soluble in alcohol or oils, insoluble in water. **Properties**: excellent emollient & moisturizer, natural sunscreen properties, antioxidant properties. **Use**: warm to melt before use, add to oil phase, use level for skin & lip care products 4-20%.

Beeswax	**Description**: bleached bees wax, cera alba, CAS# 8012-89-3. Glandular excretion product from bees, composed of myricin (>70 wax esters) & cerin (palmitinic, cerotinic & melissinic acid). White flakes, no or honey-like odor. Soluble in oils & warm alcohol, insoluble in water. Melting point 61-68°C (142-154°F). **Properties**: non-gelling thickener, emulsifier, emollient, film forming agent. **Use**: warm to 61-68°C (142-154°F), use level 2-40%.

Bismuth Oxychloride

Description: fine crystals composed of salt & bismuth (naturally occurring metallic element). CAS# 7787-59-9. Fine white crystalline powder, no odor. Insoluble in water, but miscible in oils. **Properties**: pearlescent pigment providing whiteness, lustre & brightness, good filling properties providing smooth texture. **Use**: add as is to formulas, can be blended with other pigments.

BHT

Description: butylated hydroxytoluene (BHT), CAS# 128-37-0. Synthetic antioxidant widely used as food preservative. Melting point 70°C (158°F). White crystalline powder, no odor. Water-insoluble. **Properties**: neutralizes free oxygen radicals & prevents autooxidation of organic materials (prevents rancidity of fats & oils), extends shelf-life & stabilizes colorants of cosmetics. **Use**: add to oil phase, use level 0.01-0.1%, best used in combination with EDTA.

Candelilla Wax

Description: natural plant wax extracted from the candelilla plant (Euphorbia antisyphilitica). CAS# 8006-44-8. Yellow prills, oderless. Soluble in alcohol, water-insoluble. Saponification value 43 - 65. Melting point 69-73°C (156-163°F). **Properties**: non-gelling thickener, viscosity enhancer & plastizer, compatible with most natural & synthetic waxes & resins, excellent filmforming & protecting properties, effective emollient, adds nice gloss to lipsticks. **Use**: warm to melt before use, add to oil phase.

Carnauba Wax

Description: natural plant wax exuded by the leaves of a palm tree (copernicia cerifera), hardest natural wax available, composed of wax esters (85%), free fatty acids, fatty alcohols & resins (15%). CAS# 8015-86-9. Yellow flakes or powder, no or faint odor. Soluble in alcohol, water-insoluble. Melting point 80-85°C (176-185°F). **Properties**: non-gelling thickener, viscosity enhancer, provides texture & stability due to high melting point, emollient & moisturizer, skin protectant properties. **Use**: warm to melt before use, add to oil phase.

Castor Oil

Description: ricinus oil, oleum ricini. CAS# 8001-79-4. Natural vegetable oil derived from the seeds of the herbaceous plant castor. Consists of 90% ricinoleic acid, 3-4% oleic acid, 3-4% linoleic acid. Clear slightly yellowish viscous liquid, mild odor. Miscible in alcohol, water-insoluble. **Properties**: excellent emollient & moisturizer, repairs & nourishes the hair, stimulates the scalp, gives shine to lipsticks & lipbalms. **Use**: can be added to formulas as is, add to the oil phase. Incompatible with hydorcarbons (double separation).

Ceteareth-20

Description: ceteareth-20. CAS# 68439-49-6. Non-ionic polyoxyethylene ether of cetyl/stearyl alcohol. White powder, no odor. Dissolves in water & alcohol to form a colloid solution. HLB value 15-17 (gives oil-in-water emulsions). **Properties**: universal emulsifier for o/w emulsions, compatible with all kinds of oils & active ingredients, can be combined with other emulsifiers, optimal use with gel-forming thickeners. **Use**: typical use level 0.5-3%.

Cetyl Alcohol

Description: 1-hexadecanol. CAS# 36653-82-4. Synthetic (occurs also naturally in whale oil as palmitic acid ester), composed of fatty alcohols. White flakes, no or faint odor. Soluble in water & alcohol. **Properties**: non-gelling thickener, co-emulsifier if concentration >5 %, viscosity & consistency enhancer (also in waterless products like lipsticks), emollient, moisturizer, foam booster. **Use**: melt before use (54°C, 129°F), use level 0.5-6%.

Cocoa Butter

Description: theobroma cacao seed butter. CAS# 8002-31-2. Natural fat from the seeds of the fruit of the Cacao tree, rich in oleic, stearic & palmitic fatty acids, vanillic acid, sterols, tannins & pigments. Yellow solid fat, cacao odor. Soluble in warm alcohol or oils, water-insoluble. **Properties**: skin softener & conditioner, film forming agent, thickener, moisturizer, anti-wrinkles effects. **Use**: warm to melt before use, add to oil phase, use level 3-60%.

Corn Starch AS

Description: natural sugar derived 100% from plants. Hydrophobically modified with alkenylsuccinate to enhance compatibility with oils & emulsifiers. Cross-linked with calcium salt to improve water swelling & thickening. CAS# 194810-88-3. White free-flowing powder. Water-insoluble, swells in hot water. pH Value: 5-6. **Properties**: thickener & viscosity enhancer, provides velvety feel, mitigates heavy & greasy feel of oils & waxes, can replace talc in formulas. **Use**: add as is to formulas.

CreamMaker Blend

Description: emulsifier blend of glyceryl monostearate & polyoxyethylene stearate (PEG-100 stearate). CAS No.: 123-94-4; 11099-07-3; 31566-31-1; 85666-92-8. Off-white flakes, odorless. Water-insoluble, dispersible in water & oil. Saponification value 90-100. HLB Value: 11.2. pH Value: 5.5-7 (3% solution). **Properties**: self-emulsifying blend for highly stable oil-in-water emulsions, gives excellent appearance & feel, thickening properties, stabilizes essential oils. **Use**: warm to melt before use, dispersible in water or oil.

Cyclo-methi-cone / Dimethi-cone

Description: dimethicone & cyclomethicone are both silicones (often combined). Silicones are polymers made up of oxgyen & silicon. CAS# 9006-65-9, 541-02-6. Clear, viscous liquid, odorless. Water-insoluble, soluble in alcohol, dispersible in oils & fats. **Properties**: non-greasy conditioner, provides softness & velvety feel, better spreadability of emulsions, makes colors better dispersible. **Use**: typical use level 1-10%, add to oil phase of formulas.

Edelweiss Extract

Description: high-purity extract from the Swiss alpine flower Edelweiss (leontopodium alpinum). Actives: bisabolane, sitosterol, tannin, chlorogenic acid, apigenin-7-glucoside, luteolin, luteolin-4-glucoside. Clear liquid, faint plant odor. Water-soluble. **Activity**: has twice the antioxidant activity of vitamin C! **Properties:** potent antioxidant with very effective anti-aging, anti-inflammatory & anti-septic effects, protects the skin before & after sun exposure. Skin protection is enhanced further with sun-filters. **Use:** add to formulas as is, use level: 3 - 5%.

EDTA

Description: ethylenediaminetetraacetic acid tetrasodium salt, CAS# 64-02-8. Chelating agent able to bind metal ions (e.g. sodium, calcium, magnesium, zinc). Widely used in the food and cosmetics. Off-white powder, no odor. Water-soluble. **Properties**: effective preservative (enhances efficacy of other preservatives), stabilizes pH value, emulsion and foam stabilizer, antioxidant (enhances effects of vitamin C and E). **Use**: use level 0.1-2%.

GelMaker EMU

Description: preneutralized polymer (sodium acrylate / acryloyldimethyl taurate copolymer / isohexadecane/ polysorbate 80). CAS# 77019-71-7 / 4390-04-9 / 9005-65-6. Translucent, slightly viscous liquid. pH: 5-7. **Properties**: excellent gel-forming thickener, emulsifies all kinds of oil phases incl. silicones & plant oils without a conventional emulsifier, able to produce cold emulsions, gives light & pleasant texture to spread on skin. **Use**: use level 0.5-5%, can be added to oil or water phase, or at the end of emulsification at 70-75°C.

Glycerin — **Description**: present in most cells, derived from hydrolysis of fats & fermentation of sugars. CAS# 56-81-5. Clear, slightly viscous liquid, odorless, sweet tasting. Water-soluble. **Properties**: effective moisturizer, attracts water to skin, protects skin cells, solvent for water-insoluble ingredients, good emollient & lubricant. **Use**: add as is to water phase, typical use level 2-5% in emulsions.

Grapefruit Seed Extract — **Description**: natural extract from the seeds & pulp of grapefruits, active ingredients are bioflavonoids, 60% active substances & 40% solvents (glycerine), pH 2-3 (10% solution), CAS# 90045-43-5. Viscous, bronze color, faint odor. Soluble in water. **Properties**: natural preservative preventing growth of yeasts, molds & bacteria. **Use**: can be added as is, use level 0.5-3%. For long-term preservation combination with other preservatives is recommended.

Grapeseed Oil — **Description**: natural oil pressed from the seeds of grapes, contains 60-76% linoleic acid, 12-25% oleic acid, 6-9% palmitic acid and 3-6% stearic acid, rich in vitamin A, D and E. CAS # 8024-22-4. Pale yellow to greenish liquid, faint odor. Soluble in alcohol, water-insoluble. **Properties**: excellent non-greasy emollient with good skin absorption, mild astringent effect (tightens & tones the skin), useful for acne, oily & impure skin. **Use**: use level 1-100%.

Guar Gum, Cationic — **Description**: Modified, naturally derived (from the seeds of the plant cyampopis tetragonolobus) high-molecular weight sugar. CAS# 65497-29-2. Yellowish powder, faint characteristic odor. Water-soluble. **Properties**: excellent non-gelling thickener, viscosity & foam enhancer. Compared to normal guar gum, cationic guar gum is also conditioning due to the quaternary polymer structure. **Use**: dissolve in water and stir thoroughly for 5 min, use level 0.1-2%.

Gum Arabic, Prehydrated — **Description**: acacia gum. CAS# 9000-01-5. Natural, dried exsudate from the the Acacia tree in Africa, consists of various starch molecules. Fine, white powder, faint odor. Water soluble. Prehydrated for better integration into formulas. **Properties**: o/w-emulsifier, dispersing & film-forming agent, foam & emulsion stabilizer, thickener. **Use**: add to water phase, use level 1-10 %.

HP Starch — **Description**: naturally derived, pre-gelatinized sugar (hydroxypropyl starch phosphate). Off-white free-flowing powder, soluble & swellable in cold water, pH Value: 4.5-7 (1% solution). **Properties**: stabilizes emulsions, simplifies emulsion procedure, gives conditioning after-feel, viscosity & body, reduces greasiness, imparts a smooth velvety feel in powders & makeup. **Use**: add as is to formula, typical use level is 3-10% depending on desired viscosity.

Hydrocarbons See below: isododecane, isoeicosane, isohexadecane.

Isododecane, **Description**: synthetic hydrocarbon emollients consisting of branched C12
Isoeicosane, (isododecane), C16 (isohexadecane) or C20 (isoeicosane) isoparaffins. Free
Isohexadecane of aromatics, colorless, odorless. **Properties**: non-irritant & non-comedogenic
emollients & solvents, provide non-greasy silky feel on skin, used for lipsticks,
mascara, foundation, gel blush. **Use**: add to oil phase, use level 1-10%.

Jojoba Gel **Description**: gel consisting of jojoba oil (Simmondsia chinensis) and polymers
(ethylene-propylene/butylene-styrene copolymer. CAS# 61789-91-1. Water-
insoluble, soluble in oils. Viscous pale yellow fluid, odorless. **Properties**: Gel
thickener & emollient, improves stability, thickness & visosity of emulsions &
lip care products, gives shine to lip care products, ideal to wet pigments. **Use**:
add to oil phase (lipstick, lip gloss, creams, lotions). Use level is 5-80%. Jojoba
gel is not compatible with triglyceride & silicones.

Jojoba Oil / **Description**: pure natural liquid wax (not an oil as such) derived from the
Wax seeds of a plant (simmondsia chinensis), composed of different liquid wax
esters similar to human sebaceous, based on fatty acids & fatty alcohols (no
triglycerides), cold-pressed, water-insoluble. CAS# 61789-91-1. Clear oily tan
liquid, no or faint odor. **Properties**: excellent moisturizer & emollient, anti-
wrinkle agent, good lubricant without oil film (penetrates the skin), protects
partly from UV rays (SPF about 4). **Use**: can be used as. Use level 1-50%.

Kaolin **Description**: synonyms: china clay, nacrite, kaolinite. CAS# 1332-58-7. Natural mineral (anhydrous aluminum silicate) composed of kaolinite with low iron
content, pH 5. Off-white fine powder, odorless. Water-insoluble. **Properties**:
great covering ability, able to absorb fats from the skin, refines pores & helps
clear up breakouts, soothing properties (ideal for sensitive skin). **Use**: can be
added to formulas as is, use level 4-20%.

Lanolin **Description**: Mixture of organic alcohls derived from hydrolysis of non-
Alcohol saponifiable fractions of high-purity lanolin. Melting point 50°C/32°F. Yellowish pellets. CAS# 8027-33-6. **Properties**: non-irritant, non-allergic & non-
comedogenic emollient, thickener and stabilizer, provides non-greasy feel on
the skin. **Use**: can be added to formulas as is, use level 1-20%.

Lecithin **Description**: natural lipid that occurs in most living cells, consists of four different phospholipids, capable to bind water & fats, mostly derived from soybeans. CAS# 8002-43-5. Amber-brown, honey-like with faint nutty odor. Soluble in oils, partly soluble in alcohols, dispersible in water. HLB value 4 (gives water-in-oil emulsions). **Properties**: good emulsifier with excellent water binding ability (prevents moisture loss on skin), emollient, antisticking & refatting properties, controls viscosity. **Use**: add to oil phase. Use level 1-5%.

Magnesium **Description**: magnesium octadecanoate. CAS# 557-04-0. Ester of magnesium
Stearate & stearic acid. Fine white soapy powder, faint odor of fatty acid. Soluble in warm alcohol, miscible in oils, insoluble in water. **Properties**: white coloring agent (opacifier), filling agent (provides texture), non-gelling thickener, emulsifier, film forming agent, lubricant. **Use**: for dry applications use as is, for liquid applications add to the oil phase of the formulas.

Meadowfoam **Description**: lipids & sterols from meadowfoam seed oil (limnanthes alba),
Seed Oil combined with sheabutter extract (butyrospermum parkii). CAS# 153065-40-8, 91080-23-8. Clear yellow liquid, no odor. Water-insoluble. **Properties**: excellent moisturizer due to high water absorption ability, high oxidative stability (one of the most stable oils), gives non-greasy feel, good pigment wetting properties in color cosmetics. **Use**: use level 1-100%.

Micas **Description**: natural pigment derived from the mineral Muscovite Mica, coated with titanium dioxide & iron oxide. Classified as permitted exempt color for cosmetics. Insoluble but miscible in liquids. **Properties**: gives deep color with shimmering & pearlizing lustre. **Use**: suspends best in thick bases, mixable with other pigments. No use restrictions (can be used in lip and eye area).

Mica Powder **Description**: natural shimmer pigment derived from the mineral Muscovite Mica (potassium aluminum silicate). Transparent & colorless (not coated with titanium dioxide & iron oxide). CAS# 12001-26-2. Grey-white free-flowing powder. Insoluble but miscible in water. **Properties**: texturizer for improved skin feel, increases slip & skin adhesion, bulking agent in emulsions, reduces greasiness of oil-containing formulas, can replace talc as filler, anti-caking properties. **Use**: use levels: 10-40% (as texturizer), 3-6% (used to reduce greasiness of oil-containing products).

Mica Pigments — **Description**: natural shimmer pigment derived from the mineral Muscovite Mica (potassium aluminum silicate), coated with titanium dioxide & iron oxide to create colors. Classified as permitted exempt color for cosmetics. Insoluble but miscible in liquids. **Properties**: gives deep color with shimmering & pearlizing lustre. **Use**: suspends best in thick bases, mixable with other pigments. No use restrictions (can be use in cosmetic for lip and eye area).

Mica Spheres — **Description**: fine mica combined with tiny silica beads. CAS# 7631-86-9, 12001-26-2. Fine gray powder, no odor. Insoluble, but miscible in water. **Properties**: filling agent for texture & consistency, provides extremely soft & velvet feel, improves viscosity of emulsions, decreases drying time of liquid eyeliners, improves binding of powders. **Use**: for powders use 10-25%, for liquids (e.g. liquid eyeliners, cream foundations, lotions) use 5-10%.

Microcrystalline Wax — **Description**: mineral wax consisting of hydrocarbons structured as fine crystals, derived from residium. CAS# 63231-60-7. Off-white chunks, odorless. Water-insoluble, soluble in oils. Melting point 63-68°C (145-155°F). **Properties**: ability to bind oils & solvents (prevent sweating of lipsticks), crystals insure high tensile strength & consistency (more malleable than paraffin), insures color uniformity in color cosmetics, compatible with all kinds of oils & waxes. **Use**: add to heated oil phase of formulas, typical use level 1-20%.

OM-Cinnamate — **Description**: synonyms: 2-ethylhexyl-p-methoxycinnamate, octyl methoxycinnamate (OMC), CAS# 5466-77-3. Ester of methoxycinnamate made of a derivative of cinnamic acid (occurrs in balsam of Peru, cinnamon leaves), purity >98%. Clear viscous liquid, odorless. Soluble in oil & alcohol, water insoluble. **Properties**: potent absorber of sun rays (mainly UVB, less UVA). **Use**: can be added to formulas as is, use level 2-10% (maximum allowed: USA 7.5 %, Europe & Japan 10 %). Should be stored light-protected.

Oxybenzone — **Description**: aromatic ketone (synonyms: 2-hydroxy-4-methoxy-benzophenone, benzophenone-3). CAS# 131-57-7. Pale yellow crystalline powder, weak rose-like odor. Water-insoluble, soluble in alcohol & oil. **Properties**: potent UVA & UVB absorber, protects from sun-induced skin aging (UVA), enhances UVB protection of other sunscreens, protects polymers & organic substances in cosmetic products, stabilizes color cosmetics. **Use**: incorporate into oil phase, 1.5 SPF per 1%, allowed use levels: USA 2-6 %, EU 10%, Japan 5%.

Ozokerite Wax

Description: mineral hydrocarbon wax, originally derived from veins in sandstones. CAS# 8021-55-4. White pastilles, odorless. Water-insoluble, soluble in warm oils. Melting point 73-76°C (164-169°F). **Properties**: great wax to give hardness, gel strength & consistency, insures color uniformity, emulsifying & emollient properties, compatible with all kinds of mineral & plant oils & waxes. **Use**: add to heated oil phase of formulas, typical use level 1-20%.

Paraben-DU

Description: mixture of 3% propylparaben (CAS# 94-13-3), 11% methylparaben (CAS# 99-76-3), & 30% diazolidinyl urea (CAS# 78491-02-8). Water-soluble. Clear yellowish liquid, weak odor. **Properties**: potent & mild broad spectrum biocide preventing growth of yeasts, molds & bacteria. **Use**: use level 0.3-1% dependent on the complexity of the formulation & the desired shelf-life.

PEG-7 Glyceryl Cocoate

Description: polyoxyethylene (PEG-7) glyceryl monococoate, CAS# 68201-46-7. Non-ionic, ethoxlyated polyethylene glycol ester made from glycerin & coconut oil. Clear oily liquid, characteristic odor. Soluble in water & alcohols, insoluble in oils. HLB value 11 (gives oil-in-water emulsions). **Properties**: multifunctional agent with emulsifying, emollient, refatting, conditioning & thickening properties. **Use**: can be used as is, use level 1-10%.

Petroleum Jelly (Vaseline)

Description: semi-solid mixture of hydrocarbons obtained from petroleum. CAS# 8009-03-8. Translucent paste, odorless. Water-insoluble, dispersible in oils, soluble in hot alcohol, melting point >100°F (>37°C). **Properties**: excellent emollient & lubricant , enhances consistency & viscosity (e.g. ideal bodifying agent for lip care products). **Use**: typical use level 1-20% (can also be used 100% pure on the skin).

Phenoxy-ethanol SA

Description: Blend of phenoxyethanol & sorbic acid in an emollient base of caprylyl glycol. Clear to light yellow liquid. Soluble in alcohol, insoluble in water. CAS# 122-99-6, 110-44-1. **Properties**: effective broad spectrum protection against gram-positive & gram-negative bacteria, yeast, & mold, compatible with most raw materials. **Use**: use level 0.75-1.50%, can be added directly to the formulation during pre- or post-emulsification at or below 60°C.

Polyisobutene **Description**: synthetic hydrogenated liquid isoparaffin, available at different molecular weights and viscosity. CAS# 40921-86-6, 61693-08-1. Clear liquid, no odor. Water-insoluble, soluble in oils. **Properties**: non-comedogenic & non-irritant emollient & moisturizer, restores skin suppleness, waterproofing agent, easily emulsifiable, pigment dispersing agent for color cosmetics, shine enhancer for lipcare products, improves spreadability of creams, non-greasy, for soft feel. **Use**: can be added to formulas as is, use level 1-50%.

Polysorbate 60 **Description**: Tween 60, polyoxyethylene (20) sorbitan monostearate, CAS# 9005-67-8. Synthetic, consists of sorbitol, ethylene oxide & stearic acid. Brownish viscous liquid, no or weak odor. Soluble in water & alcohols, insoluble in oils. HLB value: 14.9 (gives oil-in-water emulsions). **Properties**: non-ionic, multi-purpose emulsifier, dispersing agent, thickener antistat, solubilizer & stabilizer of essential oils. **Use**: warm to melt before use.

Polysorbate 80 **Description**: glycol, tween 80, polyoxyethylene (20) sorbitan monooleate, CAS# 9005-65-6. Synthetic, consists of sorbitol, ethylene oxide, oleic acid. Amber, viscous liquid, odorless. Soluble in water & alcohols, insoluble in oils. HLB value 15 (gives oil-in-water emulsions). **Properties**: non-ionic emulsifier, dispersing agent, solubilizer, mild antistatic & conditioning properties, solubilizer & stabilizer of essential oils. **Use**: can be used as is.

Potassium Sorbate **Description**: 2,4-hexadienoic acid potassium salt of sorbic acid (natural fatty acid). CAS # 24634-61-5. In water sorbic acid is released which is the active agent. Widely used preservative in foods & cosmetics. Fine powder, no odor. Water-soluble. **Properties**: effective preservative active against molds, yeast and aerophile bacteria. Activity further enhanced by chelating agents (e.g. EDTA). Effective in a wide pH range of 2-6.5. **Use**: typical use level 0.15-0.3% (if used alone) or 0.1-0.2% (if used with other preservatives).

Propylene Glycol **Description**: Synthetic alcohol, metabolized to lactic acid in the skin. CAS# 57-55-6. Clear, slightly viscous liquid, odorless, tasteless. Water-soluble. **Properties**: effective humectant & wetting agent preventing water loss, increases skin permeability of active ingredients as it penetrates into the skin, emollient & lubricant, excellent solubilizer of other ingredients, increases spreading of creams. **Use**: add to water phase of the formulas, typical use level 1-8%.

44

Provitamin B5 **Description**: D-panthenol, D-pantothenyl alcohol. CAS# 81-13-0. Clear viscous liquid, odorless. Soluble in water & alcohol, not in oils. **Properties**: penetrates readily skin, potent moisturizer & softener of the skin, makes the skin more elastic, soothes irritated skin (anti-inflammatory effects), heals minor wounds (promotes epithelialization). **Use**: warm to melt before use (turns water-thin), can be added to cold or hot formulas, use level 0.5-3%.

Rose Hip Oil **Description**: natural oil extracted from the seeds of the rosehip or wildrose (Rosa Aff. Rubiginosa). High in linoleic & linolenic essential fatty acids which are key components of epidermal skin cells. CAS# 8007-01-0. Clear yellowish liquid. Hardly soluble in alcohol. **Properties**: excellent emollient & moisturizer, leaves the skin soft, smooth & hydrated, helps heal scars, burns & eczema, helps to reduce wrinkles, ideal to treat distressed skin. **Use**: 1-100 %.

Sheabutter **Description**: Plant fat of the nuts of the African Karite tree (butyrospermum parkii). CAS# 91080-23-8. Contains allantoin, vitamin A & E, and cinnamic & unsaponifiable lipids. Off-white to grey-green solid fat, no or faint odor. Water-insoluble. **Properties**: potent moisturizer & emollient, provides skin protection (also partly against UV radiation), anti-inflammatory & soothing properties, anti-aging effects. **Use**: melt before use, use level 2-100%.

Sorbitan Stearate **Description**: sorbitan monostearate. CAS# 1338-41-6. Derived from sorbitol & stearic acid (from vegetable oil). Pale-yellow pellets, odorless. Partly soluble in alcohols, insoluble in water & oils. HLB value 4.7 (gives water-in-oil emulsions). **Properties**: mild all-purpose water-in-oil emulsifier (further stabilized when combined with polysorbate 60 or 80), dispersing agent, thickening properties. **Use**: warm to melt before use, use level 1-6%.

Sorbitol **Description**: Natural polyhydric alcohol derived from wheat dextrose (sugar), consists of the alcohols D-glucitol & D-mannitol, resistant to acids & alkalis, stable at temperatures up to 180°C (356°F). CAS# 50-70-4. White, crystalline powder, slightly sweet odor. Water-soluble. **Properties**: excellent thickening effects providing viscosity & texture, stabilizes gels & provides good clarity, effective moisturizing properties, good smoothing & conditioning effects. **Use**: can be added to formulas as is, use level 5-50%.

Stearic Acid **Description**: anionic emulsifier (synonym: octadecanoic acid, heptadecane carboxylic acid). Natural fatty acid occurring in vegetable fats. CAS# 57-11-4. White to yellowish flakes, oil-like odor. Water-insoluble, soluble in oils & alcohols. **Properties**: good emulsifying & thickening properties (stabilizes emulsions), gives soft waxy, pearly & cool feel on the skin. **Use**: warm to melt before use, use level 2-10%.

Stearyl Palmitate **Description:** pure vegetable ester derived from stearyl alcohol & methyl ester. CAS# 2598-99-4. Melting point 57°C (135°F), white-yellowish pellets, faint odor. Water-insoluble, soluble in oils. **Properties:** thickener with emollient properties, provides enhanced whiteness in creams & lotions, enhances emulsion stability, effective film former, reduces greasy feel of oil systems, improves payoff characteristics in stick cosmetics. **Use:** add to oil phase of formulas, use level 2-10%.

Talc **Description**: synonyms: magnesium silicate hydroxide, soap-stone, steatite. Hydrous natural mineral consisting of silicon, oxygen & magnesium, purified to remove other metals as impurities. CAS# 14807-96-6. Fine white & soft powder, faint earthy odor. Water-insoluble. **Properties**: great filling agent for powders (gives texture), non-gelling thickener, film forming agent (adheres to the skin & repels water), stabilizer of fragrances. **Use**: add as is to formulas.

Titanium Dioxide **Description**: White crystalline pigment derived from the naturally occurring mineral ilmenite. High refractive index able to reflect & scatter light, particle size 200-250nm (also available as micronized powder: 10-20nm). CAS# 13463-67-7. White powder, odorless, water-insoluble. Also available predispersed in oil. **Properties**: good texturizer with ability to absorb sun rays (UVA & UVB), whitening effect, water resistant. **Use**: can be added to formulas as is, use level 2-25 % (the higher the level, the higher the sun protection factor).

Triglyceride **Description**: caprylic / capric triglycerides . Lipid (triester) composed of glycerin, caprylic & capric fatty acids derived from coconut & palm kernel oils. CAS# 73398-61-5 / 65381-09-1. Clear oily liquid, no or faint odor. Water-insoluble. **Properties**: low-viscosity emollient & lubricant, provides non-greasy feel, improves spreading of creams, excellent vehicle & solvent for lipophilic active ingredients. **Use**: can be added to formulas as is, use level 5-50%.

Tripeptide-5   **Description**: bioactive peptide (palmitoyl tripeptide-3) able to activate tissue growth factor (TGF-beta) that stimulates collagen synthesis in the skin. Contains glycerine. Clear liquid, no odor. Easily water-soluble. **Properties**: potent stimulation of collagen synthesis in the skin, actively irons out any type of wrinkle, good skin firming & moisturizing properties, able to repair stretch marks, clinically proven to be effective & safe. Good alternate to collagen injections. **Use**: add as is at the end of formulas, use level: 1-3%.

Vitamin A   **Description**: retinol palmitate, retinyl palmitate, CAS# 79-81-2. Clear, golden oily liquid, faint odor. Product crystallizes when refrigerated for storage (warm to melt for use). Water-insoluble. **Properties**: potent skin regenerating properties (promotes epithelization & keratinization, anti-aging & anti-acneic properties. **Use**: can be added to formulas as is, use levels 500-10,000 IU/g.

Vitamin C (L-ascorbic acid)   **Descriptions**: Active form of vitamin C as it occurs in nature. CAS# 50-81-7. White powder, available as normal fine or ultrafine, odorless. Water-soluble. **Properties**: potent antioxidant (protects skin from oxidative damages), induces collagen production (improves skin elasticity), anti-inflammatory, soothing & skin-whitening effects. Effects can be increased by combining L-ascorbic acid with L-ascorbyl palmitate and/or vitamin E. **Use**: can be added to formulas as is, use level 0.2-4 %. Should be formulated at pH <3.5 for best results.

Vitamin C (L-ascorbyl palmitate)   **Description**: oil-soluble form of vitamin C. CAS# 137-66-6. White-yellowish powder, odorless. Oil-soluble, water-insoluble. Is more stable but somewhat less potent than L-ascorbic acid. **Properties** & **Use**: see L-ascorbic acid.

Vitamin E (dl-alpha-tocopheryl acetate)   **Description**: Synthetic vitamin E. CAS# 58-95-7. Clear viscous yellow liquid, faint odor. Soluble in alcohol & oil, water-insoluble. **Properties**: active only on the skin (tissue esterases must first cleave off the acetate to form active vitamin E), potent antioxidant (protects from damages by reactive oxygen radicals & UV rays), moisturizing & antiaging effect, anti-inflammatory properties, promotes epithelisation & enzyme activity. **Use**: use level 1-10%.

Vitamin E (d-alpha-to-copherol)   **Description**: Natural vitamin E. CAS# 59-02-9. Clear brown liquid, faint odor. Water-insoluble. **Properties**: primarily antioxidant in products but less active on skin, ideal to stabilize oils & fats in products. **Use**: use level 1-10%.

Xanthan Gum   **Description**: Corn sugar gum. Excretion product from bacteriae (Xanthomas campestris) composed of polysaccharides (sugars). Prehydrated forms are easier to dissolve in water. CAS# 11138-66-2. White powder, odorless. Water-soluble. **Properties**: non-gelling thickener (but binds water), viscosity, volume & foam enhancer, emulsion stabilizer, lubricant, suspending agent. **Use**: sprinkle into warm water under continuous stirring, use level 0.5-3%.

Zinc Oxide   **Description**: produced from naturally occurring zinc ore. CAS# 1314-13-2. Fine white powder, odorless. Insoluble but dispersible in water, oils & triglyceride. **Properties**: absorbs full UV spectrum (UVA & UVB), soothing effects (widely used against skin irritations), anti-fungal properties. **Use**: can be added to formulas as is, use level 5-25%. Maximum allowed: USA 25%, Japan no limit. Can be combined with other sun screens & pigments.

Foundations
& Concealers

Introduction

Traditionally, liquid foundations are used to even out skin tone, impart color, and hide skin imperfections. Newer foundations, however, may offer additional functions as sun protection, skin regeneration or anti-aging properties. By making foundations on your own, you have the possibility to create your very own multifunctional foundation, customized exactly to your needs. You have a huge variety of options to enrich your foundations with, for example, sun protection agents or active ingredients including anti-wrinkle agents, alpha-hydroxy acids, proteins, liposomes, or similar substances.

Know Your Skin

Before you start making a foundation, you should consider the following:

Skin Type: if you have an uneven skin tone, enlarged pores, skin imperfections, or scars, you should aim to make a foundation with a high opacity and coverage. If you have flawless skin with only minor imperfections, you can use a foundation with only minimal coverage or only a tinted moisturizing cream.

Skin Color: Another consideration in making a foundation is skin color. Typically, there are three major color categories: sallow (yellow-based), ruddy (red-based), and neutral (no predominance of red or yellow). These basic tones can then be mixed further with shading colors to various shades and depths.

Skin Oiliness: The formulation of your foundation should be different if you have oily, normal or dry skin. Foundations for dry to normal skin should have a significantly higher amount of emollients (e.g. oils and butters) than foundations for oily skin. For very oily skin, oil-absorbing agents such as talc, kaolin and corn starch complete the formulation. "Oil-free products" contain usually no mineral oil but they can contain plant oils, or other emollients.

Forms of Foundations

Foundations can be formulated in various forms including:

Liquid Foundations: Typically, liquid foundations are creams or gels based on either oil-in-water or water-in-oil emulsions. While oil-in-water emulsions are the preferred system, there has been a renewed interest in water-in-oil emulsions with the development of silicones. Silicone-based water-in-oil emulsions have a less greasy feel than traditional water-in-oil emulsions. Instead, silicones give a soft velvety feel on the skin.

Solid Foundations: Solid foundations include compact and stick foundations. They are often water-less formulas and contain a high proportion of low-viscosity oils, and solid esters and waxes. Typical products of such water-less formulas are foundation sticks, concealer sticks and compact cream foundations.

Tinted Cream-Gel
Light Tint, 100 ml / 3.4 floz

This is a lightweight tinted Cream-Gel for a natural look on make-up free days. The formula is rich, and blends easily giving skin a dewy, glowing look with light coverage. It is formulated with a firming and collagen boosting blend that includes hyaluronic acid and tripeptide-5. Sun protection factor is 10-14.

Method: Add phase A into a glass beaker and blend well. Add phase B into another glass beaker and blend well. Add the distilled water of phase C into another vessel, sprinkle the hyaluronic acid into the water and stir thoroughly with a hand mixer to avoid the formation of lumps. Add phase C to phase B and blend well. Add phase A to phase B/C and mix well until uniform. Add phase D to phase A/B/C and stir well. Fill into jars or tubes.

Phase A
OM-Cinnamate 5% (5ml / 1tsp)
Triglyceride 8.5% (8.5ml / 1/2Tbsp)
GelMaker EMU 3% (3ml / 1/2tsp)
Corn Starch AS 4% (4g / 2tsp)
Pigment Blend Dispersion 1% (1ml / 1/4tsp)
Vitamin E Acetate 0.5% (0.5ml / 12drops)

Phase B
Distilled Water 10% (10ml / 2tsp)
PEG-7 Glyceryl Cocoate 1.5% (1.5ml / 36 drops)
Glycerin 2% (2ml / 1/2tsp)
Titanium Dioxide 2% (2g / 3/4tsp)

Phase C
Distilled Water 57.1% (57.1ml / 1/4cup)
Hyaluronic Acid 0.5% (0.4g / 1/8tsp)
EDTA 0.2% (0.2g / 1/16tsp)

Phase D
Tripeptide-5 3% (3ml / 1/2tsp)
Phenoxyethanol/SA 1.5% (1.5ml / 36 drops)
Fragrance (optional) 0.2% (0.2ml / 5 drops)

Tinted Cream-Gel with Bronze Sparkles
Deep Tint, 100 ml / 3.4 floz

This light tinted moisturizing Cream-Gel has a tan color for the darker skin type. It has a smooth texture, is absorbed quickly and moisturizes the skin well. It is formulated with a firming and collagen boosting blend that includes hyaluronic acid and tripeptide-5. Sun protection factor is 12-15.

Method: Add phase A into a glass beaker and blend well. Add the distilled water of phase B into another glass beaker, sprinkle the hyaluronic acid into the water and stir thoroughly with a little hand mixer to avoid the formation of lumps. Add phase C to phase B and blend well. Add phase A to phase B/C, blend well until uniform. Add phase D to phase A/B/C and stir again well. Fill into jars or tubes.

Phase A
OM-Cinnamate 7.5% (5ml / 1tsp)
Jojoba Oil 8% (8ml / 1/2Tbsp)
GelMaker 3% (3ml / 1/2tsp + 1/8tsp)
Corn Starch AS 3.5% (3.5g / 1 3/4tsp)
Pigment Blend Dispersion 2.5% (2.5ml / 1/2tsp)
Vitamin E Acetate 0.5% (0.5ml / 12drops)

Phase B
Distilled Water 64.6% (64.6ml / 1/4cup + 1tsp)
Hyaluronic Acid 0.5% (0.5g / 1/8tsp)

Phase C
PEG-7 Glyceryl Cocoate 1.5% (1.5ml / 36 drops)
Glycerin 2% (2ml / 1/2tsp)
EDTA 0.2% (0.2g / 1/16tsp)

Phase D
Tripeptide-5 3% (3ml / 1/2tsp)
Phenoxyethanol-SA 1.5% (1ml / 36 drops)
Mica Bronze 1.5% (1.5g / 3/4tsp)
Fragrance (optional) 0.2% (0.2ml / 5 drops)

Tightening Color Corrector
Color: Green, 100 ml / 3.4 floz

This light cream is applied under makeup to hide red blotchy areas. It contains a green mica pigment to tone down the redness. It is formulated with SkinTight AP (algae extract & pullulan) for an immediate skin tightening and also long-term firming effect by protecting skin cells from oxidative stress.

Method: Add phase A into a heat resistant glass beaker. Add phase B into another heat resistant glass beaker. Heat both beakers to 160°F/71°C to melt the ingredients. Add phase A to phase B, stir well and remove from heat, blend well until uniform. Cool to 100°F/40°C and add phase C, stir well. Adjust thickness further with GelMaker EMU and color with green mica after the cream has been completed. Fill into dispenser bottles.

Phase A
Triglyceride 6.5% (6.5ml / 1 1/4tsp)
Meadowfoam Seed Oil 4% (4ml / 1tsp)
CreamMaker Blend 1.5% (1.5g / 1/2tsp)

Phase B
Distilled Water 70% (70ml / 1/4cup + 2tsp)
Glycerin 3% (3ml / 1/2tsp)
Mica Spheres 6% (6g / 1 1/2Tbsp)
Cetyl Alcohol 1.5% (1.5g / 1/2tsp)
Mica Majestic Green 1% (1g / 1/2tsp)

Phase C
GelMaker EMU 1% (1ml / 1/4tsp)
SkinTight AP 4% (4ml / 3/4tsp)
Phenoxyethanol-SA 1.5% (1.5ml / 36 drops)

Creamy Foundation (I)
Color: Pale Beige, 100 ml / 3.4 floz

Light and creamy foundation that can be applied like a moisturizer. It gives medium coverage, evens out skin tone and leaves a pleasant non-oily feel. Formulated with Tripeptide-5 that stimulates collagen synthesis and actively reduces wrinkles, firms and moisturizes the skin. Sun protection factor is 10-14.

Method: Add phase C into a mortar and blend well with the pestle until the color is uniform; test color on white paper for streaking. Add phase A into a heat resistant glass beaker. Add phase B into another heat resistant glass beaker and stir. Heat both beakers to 160°F/71°C to heat and melt the ingredients. Add phase C to phase B and stir well. Add phase A to phase B/C and stir well to form the cream. Remove from heat and stir. Cool to 100°F/40°C and add phase D, stir again well. Fill into dispenser bottle.

Phase A
Triglyceride 6% (6ml / 1 1/4tsp)
OM-Cinnamate 5% (5ml / 1tsp)
Isoeicosane 3% (3ml / 1/2tsp)
CreamMaker Blend 3% (3g / 1 1/4tsp)
Sheabutter 2% (2g / 1/2tsp)

Phase B
Distilled Water 59.9% (59.9ml / 1/4cup)
Glycerin 4% (4ml / 3/4tsp)
HP Starch 2.5% (2.5g / 3/4tsp)
Polysorbate 80 0.2% (0.2ml / 5 drops)

Phase C
Titanium Dioxide 5% (5g / 1 1/2tsp)
Pigment Blend Bare Neutral 2% (2g / 3/4tsp)
Pigment Blend Warm Beige 2% (2g / 3/4tsp)

Phase D
Tripeptide-5 3% (3ml / little over 1/2tsp)
GelMaker EMU 0.5% (0.5ml / 12 drops)
Vitamin E Tocopherol 0.2% (0.2ml / 5 drops)
Phenoxyethanol-SA 1.5% (1.5ml / 36 drops)
Fragrance (optional) 0.2% (0.2ml / 5 drops)

Creamy Foundation (II)
Dark Tan, 100 ml / 3.4 floz

Light, creamy foundation that can be applied like a moisturizer. It gives medium coverage, evens out skin tone and leaves a pleasant non-oily feel. Formulated with Edelweiss extract as a powerful antioxidant to protect the skin cells from being damaged and slows down the aging process. Sun protection factor is 8-12.

Method: Add phase C into a mortar and blend well with the pestle until the color is uniform; test color on white paper for streaking. Add phase A into a heat resistant glass beaker. Add phase B into another heat resistant glass beaker, and stir. Heat both beakers to 160°F/71°C to heat and melt the ingredients. Add phase C to phase B and stir well. Add phase A to phase B/C and stir well to form the cream. Remove from heat and stir. Cool to 100°F/40°C and add phase D, stir again well. Fill into dispenser bottle.

Phase A
Triglyceride 6% (6ml / 1 1/4tsp)
OM-Cinnamate 5% (5ml / 1tsp)
Isoeicosane 3% (3ml / 1/2tsp)
Avocado Butter 2% (2g / 1/2tsp)
CreamMaker Blend 3% (3g / 1 1/4tsp)

Phase B
Distilled Water
   62.9% (62.9ml / 1/4cup + 1/2tsp)
Glycerin 4% (4ml / 3/4tsp)
HP Starch 2.5% (2.5g / 3/4tsp)
Polysorbate 80 0.2% (0.2ml / 5 drops)

Phase C
Titanium Dioxide 2% (2g / 1/2tsp)
Pigment Blend Dark Brown 2% (2g / 3/4tsp)
Pigment Blend Caramel 3% (3g / 1tsp)

Phase D
Edelweiss Extract 2% (2ml / 1/2tsp)
GelMaker EMU 0.5% (0.5ml / 12 drops)
Vitamin E Tocopherol 0.2% (0.2ml / 5 drops)
Phenoxyethanol-SA 1.5% (1.5ml / 36 drops)
Fragrance (optional) 0.2% (0.2ml / 5 drops)

Smooth Foundation (I)
Color: Bare Neutral, 100 ml / 3.4 floz

This is an anionic soap-based emulsion which has nice application attributes and feel. Most oil-in-water foundations on the market fall into this category. The anionic emulsifier is stearic acid and is neutralized with triethanolamine. The foundation provides medium coverage, is light in texture and non-oily. Hyaluronic acid is a potent moisturizer. Lacto-ceramide restores ceramides in the skin. Mica spheres diminish the appearance of fine lines and wrinkles. OM-cinnamate and titanium dioxide provide sun protection (SPF 8-12).

Method: Add phase A into a heat resistant glass beaker and stir. Add phase B into a mortar and blend well with the pestle until the color is uniform. Test on white paper for color streaking. Add phase B to phase A and stir. Sprinkle phase C into phase A/B while stirring well. Add phase D into a heat resistant glass beaker, stir. Heat both glass beakers to 160°F/71°C to heat and melt the ingredients. Add phase D to phase A/B/C and stir well until uniform. The color can still be adjusted with pigment blend. Remove from heat, stir and cool to 100°F/40°C. Then add phase E one by one. Fill into tubes or treatment pumps.

Phase A
Distilled Water 53.2% (53.2ml / 3 1/2Tbsp)
Glycerin 2% (2ml / 1/2tsp)
Polysorbate 80 0.3% (0.3ml / 7 drops)
Triethanolamine 0.6% (0.6ml / 14 drops)

Phase B
Titanium Dioxide 5% (5g / 1 1/2tsp)
Pigment Blend Bare Neutral
  4.5% (4.5g / 1/2Tbsp)
Mica Spheres 8% 8g/2Tbsp

Phase C
Hyaluronic Acid 0.2% (0.2g / 1/4tsp)
Xanthan Gum 0.5% (0.5g / 1/4tsp)

Phase D
Triglyceride 10.5% (10.5ml / 2tsp)
OM-Cinnamate 5% (5ml / 1tsp)
Stearic Acid 2.5% (2.5g / 1tsp)
CreamMaker Blend 1.5% (1.5g / 1/2tsp)
Cetyl Alcohol 1.5% (1.5g / 1/2tsp)
Vitamin E Acetate 0.5% (0.5ml / 12 drops)

Phase E
Lacto-Ceramide 3% (3ml / 1/2tsp)
Paraben-DU 1% (1ml / 24 drops)
Fragrance (optional) 0.2% (0.2ml / 5 drops)

Smooth Foundation (II)
Color: Warm Beige, 100 ml / 3.4 floz

Light oil-in-water foundation based on an anionic emulsion as recipe on page 55. It is very pleasant to apply, hydrates the skin and delivers a soft finish. Formulated with hyaluronic acid and lacto-ceramide to deeply moisturize and restore the skin with ceramides. Mica spheres diminish the appearance of fine lines and wrinkles. The formula combines a powder pigment blend and a pigment dispersion. The dispersion gives a reddish undertone while the pigment blend a yellow one. Golden mica (optional) will give a subtle glow.

Method: Add phase A into a heat resistant glass beaker and stir. Add phase B into a mortar and blend well with the pestle until the color is uniform. Test on white paper for color streaking. Add phase B to phase A and stir. Sprinkle phase C into phase A/B while stirring well. Add phase D into a heat resistant glass beaker, stir. Heat both glass beakers to 160°F/71°C to melt the ingredients. Add phase D to phase A/B/C and stir well until uniform. The color can still be adjusted with pigment blend or pigment dispersion. Add titanium dioxide to make it lighter (needs to be predispersed). Remove from heat, stir and cool to 100°F/40°C. Then add phase E one by one. Fill into tubes or treatment pumps.

Phase A
Distilled Water 53.7% (53.7ml / 3 1/2Tbsp)
Glycerin 2% (2ml / 1/2tsp)
Polysorbate 80 0.3% (0.3ml / 7 drops)
Triethanolamine 0.6% (0.6ml / 14 drops)

Phase B
Titanium Dioxide 5% (7g / 2tsp)
Mica Spheres 6% (6g / 1 1/2Tbsp)
Pigment Blend Warm Beige
   3.5% (3.5g / 1 1/4tsp)

Phase C
Hyaluronic Acid 0.2% (0.2g / 1/4tsp)
Xanthan Gum 0.5% (0.5g / 1/4tsp)

Phase D
Medowfoam Seed Oil 6% (6ml / 1 1/4tsp)
Triglyceride 9% (9ml / 2tsp)

Stearic Acid 2.5% (2.5g / 1tsp)
Iron Oxide Brown Dispersion
   1% (1ml / 24 drops)
CreamMaker Blend 1.5% (1.5g / 1/2tsp)
Cetyl Alcohol 1.5% (1.5g / 1/2tsp)
Vitamin E Acetate 0.5% (0.5ml / 12 drops)

Phase E
Lacto-Ceramide 3% (3ml / 1/2tsp)
Mica Gold (optional) 2% (2g / 1tsp)
Paraben-DU 1% (1ml / 24 drops)
Fragrance (optional) 0.2% (0.2ml / 5 drops)

Smooth Foundation (III)
Color: Bronze Tan, 100 ml / 3.4 floz

Very similar, elegant oil-in-water foundation as the previous two recipes but with isoeicosane as emollient and darker pigments for the medium dark skin tone. Formulated with hyaluronic acid and lacto-ceramide to deeply moisturize and restore the skin with ceramides. Mica spheres diminish the appearance of fine lines and wrinkles.

Method: Add phase A into a heat resistant glass beaker and stir. Add phase B into a mortar and blend well with the pestle until the color is uniform. Test on white paper for color streaking. Add phase B to phase A and stir. Sprinkle phase C into phase A/B while stirring well. Add phase D into a heat resistant glass beaker, stir. Heat both glass beakers to 160°F/71°C to heat and melt the ingredients. Add phase D to phase A/B/C and stir well until uniform. The color can still be adjusted with pigment blend or pigment dispersion. Add titanium dioxide to make it lighter but it needs to be pre-dispersed first. Remove from heat, stir and cool to 100°F/40°C. Then add phase E one by one, stirring after each ingredient. Store in tubes or treatment pumps.

Phase A
Distilled Water 57.2% (57.2ml / 3 3/4Tbsp)
Glycerin 2% (2ml / 1/2tsp)
Polysorbate 80 0.3% (0.3ml / 7 drops)
Triethanolamine 0.6% (0.6ml / 14 drops)

Phase B
Titanium Dioxide 2% (2g / 1/2tsp)
Pigment Blend Caramel 3% (3g / 1 1/4tsp)
Pigment Blend Dark Brown 2% (2g / 3/4tsp)
Mica Spheres 5% (5g / 1Tbsp + 1tsp)
Mica Bronze (optional) 3% (3g / 1 1/2tsp)

Phase C
Hyaluronic Acid 0.2% (0.2g / 1/4tsp)
Xanthan Gum 0.5% (0.5g / 1/4tsp)

Phase D
Triglyceride 8% (8ml / 1/2Tbsp)
Isoeicosane 6% (6ml / 1 1/4tsp)
Stearic Acid 2.5% (2.5g / 1tsp)
CreamMaker Blend 1.5% (1.5g / 1/2tsp)
Cetyl Alcohol 1.5% (1.5g / 1/2tsp)
Vitamin E Acetate 0.5% (0.5ml / 12 drops)

Phase E
Lacto-Ceramide 3% (3ml / 1/2tsp)
Paraben-DU 1% (1ml / 24 drops)
Fragrance (optional) 0.2% (0.2ml / 5 drops)

Cream-to-Powder Foundation (I)

Color: Honey, 100 ml / 3.4 floz

Foundation that is poured hot and becomes creamy solid when cooled down. It will 'melt' to a creamy consistency when rubbed off with fingers and spreads well on the skin leaving a powdery finish. Easily blendable for long lasting true color. Loose Powder can be applied as a finishing touch.

Method: Add phase A into a heat resistant glass beaker. Add phase B into a mortar and blend well with the pestle until the color is uniform. Test on white paper for color streak-ing. Adjust color with iron oxide pigments and titanium dioxide until desired shade is achieved, if necessary. Add phase C to phase B and blend well with the pestle. Heat phase A to 176°F/80°C to melt the waxes, stir. Add phase B/C to phase A and stir until uniform. Remove from heat and add phase D, fill into jars or compacts. Foundation may slightly harden within couple weeks. If too solid, balance with more emollients. If too soft, add some more mica powder.

Phase A
Triglyceride 26.1% (26.1g / 1 3/4Tbsp)
Meadowfoam Seed Oil 10% (10g / 2tsp)
Sheabutter 2% (2g / 1/2tsp)
Cetyl Alcohol 5% (5g / 2tsp)
Isoeicosane 4% (4g / 3/4tsp)
Carnauba Wax 4% (4g / 1 3/4tsp)
Microcrystalline Wax 2% (2g / 3/4tsp)
Vitamin E Acetate 0.5% (0.5ml / 12 drops)
Lecithin 0.2% (0.2ml / 5 drops)

Phase B
Titanium Dioxide 13% (13g / 1Tbsp + 1tsp)
Iron Oxide Yellow 2% (2g / 1 1/2tsp)
Iron Oxide Red 0.8% (0.8g / 1/4tsp)
Iron Oxide Black 0.6% (0.6g / 1/4tsp)

Phase C
Talc 14% (14g / 1 3/4Tbsp)
Mica Spheres 14.4% (14.4g / 3Tbsp + 1 1/2tsp)

Phase D
Vitamin E Tocopherol 0.2% (0.2ml / 5 drops)
Fragrance 0.2% (0.2ml / 5 drops)
Phenoxyethanol-SA 1% (1ml / 24 drops)

Cream-to-Powder Foundation (II)
Color: Warm Beige, 100 ml / 3.4 floz

Foundation that is poured hot and becomes creamy solid when cooled down. It will 'melt' to a creamy consistency when rubbed off with fingers and spreads well on the skin leaving a powdery finish. Easily blendable for long lasting true color. Loose Powder can be applied as a finishing touch.

Method: Add phase A into a heat resistant glass beaker. Add phase B into a mortar and blend well with the pestle until the color is uniform. Test on white paper for color streaking. Adjust color with pigment blend or titanium dioxide (to make it lighter), if necessary. Add phase C to phase B and blend well with the pestle. Heat phase A to 176°F/80°C to melt the waxes, stir. Add phase B/C to phase A and stir until uniform. Remove from heat and add phase D, fill into jars or compacts. Foundation may slightly harden within couple weeks. If too solid, balance with more emollients. If too soft, add some more mica powder.

Phase A
Triglyceride 26.1% (26.1g / 1 3/4Tbsp)
Meadowfoam Seed Oil 10% (10g / 2tsp)
Sheabutter 2% (2g / 1/2tsp)
Cetyl Alcohol 5% (5g / 2tsp)
Isoeicosane 4% (4g / 3/4tsp)
Carnauba Wax 4% (4g / 1 3/4tsp)
Microcrystalline Wax 2% (2g / 3/4tsp)
Vitamin E Acetate 0.5% (0.5ml / 12 drops)
Lecithin 0.2% (0.2ml / 5 drops)

Phase B
Titanium Dioxide 11% (11g / 1Tbsp + 1/4tsp)
Pigment Blend Warm Beige 5% (5g / 2tsp)

Phase C
Talc 14% (14g / 1 3/4Tbsp)
Mica Spheres 14.8% (14.8g / 3 3/4Tbsp)

Phase D
Vitamin E Tocopherol 0.2% (0.2ml / 5 drops)
Fragrance 0.2% (0.2ml / 5 drops)
Phenoxyethanol-SA 1% (1ml / 24 drops)

Cream-to-Powder Foundation (III)
Color: Natural, 100 ml / 3.4 floz

Foundation that is poured hot and becomes creamy solid when cooled down. It will 'melt' to a creamy consistency when rubbed off with fingers and spreads well on the skin leaving a powdery finish. Easily blendable for long lasting true color. Loose Powder can be applied as a finishing touch.

Method: Add phase A into a heat resistant glass beaker. Add phase B into a mortar and blend well with the pestle until the color is uniform. Test on white paper for color streaking. Adjust color with pigment blend and/or pigment dispersion if necessary. Add phase C to phase B and blend well with the pestle. Heat phase A to 176°F/80°C to melt the waxes, stir. Add phase B/C to phase A and stir until uniform. Remove from heat and add phase D, fill into jars or compacts. Foundation may slightly harden within couple weeks. If too solid, balance with more emollients. If too soft, add some more mica powder.

Phase A
Triglyceride 26.1% (26.1g / 1 3/4Tbsp)
Meadowfoam Seed Oil 10% (10g / 2tsp)
Sheabutter 2% (2g / 1/2tsp)
Cetyl Alcohol 5% (5g / 2tsp)
Isoeicosane 4% (4g / 3/4tsp)
Carnauba Wax 4% (4g / 1 3/4tsp)
Microcrystalline Wax 2% (2g / 3/4tsp)
Vitamin E Acetate 0.5% (0.5ml / 12 drops)
Lecithin 0.2% (0.2ml / 5 drops)
Iron Oxide Brown Dispersion
    1% (1ml / 1/4tsp)

Phase B
Titanium Dioxide 9% (9g / 3/4Tbsp)
Pigment Blend Bare Beige 3% (3g / 1 1/2tsp)

Phase C
Talc 14% (14g / 1 3/4Tbsp)
Mica Spheres 17.8% (17.8g / 4 1/2Tbsp)

Phase D
Vitamin E Tocopherol 0.2% (0.2ml / 5 drops)
Fragrance 0.2% (0.2ml / 5 drops)
Phenoxyethanol-SA 1% (1ml / 24 drops)

Foundation Stick (I)
Color: Natural Buff, 100 g / 3.6 oz

Foundation sticks are popular and easy to make. They are easy to apply and blend all over the face or just where you need it. The emollients used are non-greasy and do not leave the skin oily. Contains vitamin E acetate for antioxidant protection.

Method: Add phase B into a mortar and blend well with the pestle until the color is uniform. Test on white paper for color streak-ing. Adjust color if necessary. Add phase C to phase B and blend well with the pestle. Add phase A to a heat resistant glass beaker and heat to 176°F/80°C to melt the waxes. Add phase B/C to phase A and blend well until uniform. Remove from heat, add phase D, stir and fill into stick containers. If the stick is too solid balance with more emollients; if too soft, add some more talc.

Phase A
Jojoba Oil 9% (9ml / 2tsp)
Triglyceride 24% (24ml / 5tsp)
Isoeicosane 10% (10ml / 2tsp)
Stearyl Palmitate 4% (4g / 1/2Tbsp)
Carnauba Wax 4% (4g / 1 3/4tsp)
Lecithin 0.2% (0.2g / 5 drops)
Microcrystalline Wax 3% (3g / 1 1/4tsp)
Vitamin E Acetate 1% (1ml / 24 drops)

Phase B
Titanium Dioxide 10% (10g / 1Tbsp)
Pigment Blend Natural Buff 4% (4g / 1/2Tbsp)

Phase C
Talc 12% (12g / 1 1/2Tbsp)
Mica Spheres 17.6% (17.6g / 4Tbsp + 1tsp)

Phase D
Vitamin E Tocopherol 0.2% (0.2g / 5 drops)
Phenoxyethanol-SA 1% (1ml / 24 drops)

Foundation Stick (II)

Color: Sand, 100 g / 3.6 oz

Sand-colored foundation stick that is easy to apply and blends all over the face or just where you need it. The emollients used are non-greasy and do not leave the skin oily. Contains vitamin E acetate for antioxidant protection. The iron oxide pigment blend gives a base color and blends well with the beige tone pigment blend.

Method: Add phase B into a mortar and blend well with the pestle until the color is uniform. Test on white paper for color streak-ing. Adjust color if necessary with pigment blend or pigment dispersion. Add phase C to phase B and blend well with the pestle. Add phase A to a heat resistant glass beaker and heat to 176°F/80°C to melt the waxes. Add phase B/C to phase A and blend well until uniform. Remove from heat, add phase D, stir and fill into stick containers. If the stick is too solid balance with more emollients. If too soft, add some more talc.

Phase A
Meadowfoam Seed Oil 9% (9ml / 2tsp)
Triglyceride 23% (24ml / 4 1/2tsp)
Isoeicosane 10% (10ml / 2tsp)
Stearyl Palmitate 4% (4g / 1/2Tbsp)
Carnauba Wax 4% (4g / 1 3/4tsp)
Lecithin 0.2% (0.2g / 5 drops)
Microcrystalline Wax 3% (3g / 1 1/4tsp)
Vitamin E Acetate 1% (1ml / 24 drops)
Iron Oxide Brown Dispersion 1% (1ml / 1/4tsp)
Vitamin E Acetate 1% (1ml / 24 drops)

Phase B
Titanium Dioxide 10% (10g / 1Tbsp)
Pigment Blend Warm Beige 4% (4g / 1/2Tbsp)

Phase C
Talc 10% (10g / 1Tbsp + 1/2tsp)
Mica Spheres 18.6% (18.6g / 4 1/2Tbsp)

Phase D
Vitamin E Tocopherol 0.2% (0.2g / 5 drops)
Phenoxyethanol/SA 1% (1ml / 24 drops)

Foundation Stick (III)

Color: Chestnut, 100 g / 3.6 oz

This recipe contains emollients that suit the drier skin. It blends all over the face or just where you need it. Finely dispersed iron oxide pigments are used which contain three different pigments. Foundation is formulated with protective vitamin E acetate and moisturizing sheabutter.

Method: Add phase B into a mortar and blend with the pestle until well mixed. Then add phase C to the mortar and blend well. Add phase A to a heat resistant glass beaker and heat to 176°F/80°C. Add phase B/C to phase A and blend well until uniform. Adjust color if necessary with pigment dispersion or bronze mica. Remove from heat and add phase D. Fill while hot into stick containers. If the stick is too solid, balance with more emollients; if too soft, add some more talc.

Phase A
Jojoba Oil 6% (9ml / 1 1/4tsp)
Triglyceride 20% (20ml / 4 tsp)
Isoeicosane 12% (12ml / 2 1/2tsp)
Stearyl Palmitate 4% (4g / 1/2Tbsp)
Carnauba Wax 4% (4g / 1 3/4tsp)
Sheabutter 2% (2g / 1/2tsp)
Lecithin 0.2% (0.2g / 5 drops)
Microcrystalline Wax 3% (3g / 1 1/4tsp)
Vitamin E Acetate 1% (1ml / 24 drops)
Iron Oxide Brown Dispersion 4% (4ml / 3/4tsp)
Vitamin E Acetate 1% (1ml / 24 drops)

Phase B
Talc 10% (10g / 1Tbsp)
Titanium Dioxide 4% (4g / 1 1/4tsp)

Phase C
Mica Spheres 17.6% (17.6g / 4Tbsp + 1tsp)
Mica Powder 10% (10g / 3Tbsp + 1tsp)
Mica Bronze 4% (4g / 2tsp)

Phase D
Vitamin E Tocopherol 0.2% (0.2g / 5 drops)
Phenoxyethanol-SA 1% (1ml / 24 drops)

Creamy Concealer "Tri-Colore"
Color: Pale Beige / Natural, 100 g / 3.6 oz

Concealers are similar to stick foundations but give more coverage due to the higher amount of titanium dioxide. The formula is filled with skin conditioning ingredients like vitamin A which helps minimize the appearance of fine dry lines and wrinkles. Vitamin E moisturizes and provides antioxidant protection. The recipe will give three different colors, so that you can mix your own personal shades.

Method: Add phase A into a heat resistant glass beaker. Add phase B to a mortar and blend with the pestle until the color is uniform. Test on white paper for color streaking. Add phase C to the mortar and blend well. Adjust color if necessary. Heat phase A to 176°F/80°C to melt the waxes, stir. Add phase B/C to phase A and stir until uniform. Remove from heat, add phase D to phase A/B, stir and fill while still hot into containers. If the concealer is too solid balance it with more emollients. If it is too soft stabilize it with stearyl palmitate.

For additional colors: fill only one container and leave a rest in the beaker. Add a few drops of iron oxide dispersion to the rest in the beaker, stir and fill the second container. Then add again a few more drops of iron oxide dispersion and fill the third container.

Phase A
Isoeicosane 15% (15ml / 1Tbsp)
Triglyceride 29% (29ml / 2Tbsp)
Rose Hip Oil 15% (15ml / 1Tbsp)
Ozokerite Wax 6% (6g / 2 1/3tsp)
Candelilla Wax 3% (3g / 1tsp)
Stearyl Palmitate 2% (2g / 3/4tsp)
Vitamin A Palmitate 0.5% (0.5ml / 12 drops)

Phase B
Titanium Dioxide 12% (12g / 1Tbsp + 1/2tsp)
Iron Oxide Red 0.3% (0.3g / 1/16tsp)
Iron Oxide Yellow 0.8% (0.8g / 1/2tsp)
Iron Oxide Black 0.1% (0.1g / <1/16tsp)

Phase C
Corn Starch AS 6% (6g / 1 3/4tsp)
Mica Spheres 9.8% (9.1g / 2 Tbsp + 1/2tsp)

Phase D
Tocopherol 0.2% (0.2ml / 5 drops)
Phenoxyethanol-SA 1% (1ml / 24 drops)

Creamy Concealer (II)
Color: Beach, 50 g / 1.8 oz

Creamy concealer that provides full, but natural looking coverage. The formula is enriched with various skin conditioning vitamins like vitamin A which helps minimize the appearance of fine lines and wrinkles, and vitamin E and vitamin C which both moisturize and provide antioxidant protection.

Method: Add phase B into a mortar and blend well with the pestle until the color is uniform. Test for color streaking. Add phase C to phase B and blend well, adjust color if necessary. Add phase A into a heat resistant glass beaker and heat to 168°F/76°C until the waxes are melted. Add phase B/C to phase A and blend well until uniform. Remove from heat, add phase D, stir and fill while still hot into containers. If the concealer is too solid, balance it with more emollients. If it is too soft, stabilize it with stearyl palmitate.

Phase A
Isoeicosane 12% (6ml / 1 1/4tsp)
Triglyceride 35% (17.5ml / 1Tbsp + 1/2tsp)
Ozokerite Wax 8% (4g / 1 1/2tsp)
Stearyl Palmitate Ester 2% (1g / 1/2tsp)
Sheabutter 2% (1g / 1/4tsp)
Vitamin C L-Ascorbyl Palmitate
   0.5% (0.25g / 1/8tsp)
Vitamin E Acetate 0.5% (0.25ml / 6 drops)
Lecithin 0.5% (0.25ml / 6 drops)

Phase B
Titanium Dioxide 14% (7g / 2tsp)
Iron Oxide Brown Dispersion
   0.5% (0.25ml / 6 drops)
Iron Oxide Yellow 0.7% (0.35g / 1/4tsp)
Ultramarine Blue (optional, reduces redness
   if too red) 0.1% (0.05g / < 1/16tsp)

Phase C
Mica Spheres 14.5% (7.25g / 1 3/4Tbsp)
Corn Starch AS 8% (4g / 1 1/4tsp)

Phase D
Vitamin E Tocopherol 0.2% (0.1 ml / 2 drops)
Vitamin A Palmitate 0.5% (0.25ml / 6 drops)
Phenoxyethanol-SA 1% (0.5ml / 12 drops)

Creamy Concealer (III)
Color: Caramel, 50 g / 1.8 oz

The creamy consistency of this concealer goes on smoothly, providing natural looking coverage. It contains vitamin A which helps minimize the appearance of fine lines and wrinkles, and vitamin E and C which moisturize and provide antioxidant protection.

Method: Add phase B into a mortar and blend well with the pestle until the color is uniform. Test on white paper for color streaking. Add phase C to the mortar and blend well, adjust color if necessary. Add phase A into heat resistant glass beaker and heat to 168°F/76°C until the waxes are melted. Add phase B/C to phase A and blend well until uniform. Remove from heat, add phase D stir and fill while still hot into containers.

For additional colors: fill only one container and leave a rest in the beaker. Add a few drops of iron oxide dispersion to the rest in the beaker, stir and fill the second container. Then add again a few more drops of iron oxide dispersion and fill the third container.

Phase A
Isoeicosane 10.3% (5.2g / 1 1/4tsp)
Triglyceride 35% (17.5ml / 1Tbsp + 1/2tsp)
Ozokerite Wax 8% (4g / 1/2Tbsp)
Stearyl Palmitate 2% (1g / 1/2tsp)
Vitamin C L-Ascorbyl Palmitate
  0.5% (0.25g / 1/8tsp)

Phase B
Titanium Dioxide 4% (2g / 1/2tsp)
Pigment Blend Caramel 3% (1.5g / 3/4tsp)
Pigment Blend Dark Brown 1.5% (0.75g / 3/8tsp)

Phase C
Corn Starch AS 12% (6g / 2tsp)
Mica Powder 15% (7.5g / 2 1/2Tbsp)
Mica Spheres 7% (3.5g / 1Tbsp)

Phase D
Vitamin A Palmitate 0.5% (0.25ml / 6 drops)
Vitamin E Tocopherol 0.2% (0.1ml / 2 drops)
Phenoxyethanol-SA 1% (0.5ml / 12 drops)

Makeup Remover
100 ml / 3.4 floz

Gentle formula with excellent makeup removing properties and without irritating the skin and eyes. Meadowfoam seed oil is a very stable oil that is combined with shea butter for extra moisture.

Method: Add phase A into a glass beaker and stir. Add phase B and stir well but gently to blend the ingredients. Apply to a cotton pad and wipe gently over face. For removing eye makeup, hold cotton pad over closed lids to soften mascara then wipe gently. Can also be used on a damp cotton pad.

Phase A
Polyglucose 10% (10ml / 2tsp)
Meadowfoam Seed Oil 80% (80ml / 5 1/2Tbsp)

Phase B
Distilled Water 10% (10ml / 2tsp)
Fragrance (optional) 0.2% (0.2ml / 5 drops)

Face Powders
& Mineral Makeup

Introduction

Cosmetic powders include a huge variety of products such as face powder, mineral makeup powder, blush, eye brow powder, and body powder. As there are also various multifunctional powders, it is increasingly difficult to make a clear categorization of makeup powders. In this chapter, face powders (either loose or compact), mineral makeup, and bronzing powder is discussed. Blush powders are discussed in the next chapter.

has therefore become increasingly popular over the last few years. Ideally, face powders should have the following properties:
• **Good Coverage**: Should be able to cover skin imperfections and uneven skin tones.
• **Good Adhesiveness**: Should stay on the skin and not fall off.
• **Good Absorption**: Should absorb oil and fat to provide a matte effect and avoid shine.
• **Good Slip**: Should be smooth to apply without drag and able to be spread well.

Forms of Powders

Face Powder: Makeup powder is essential to help set the foundation and provide a grease-free surface for the rest of the makeup. It gives a natural finish to the skin and helps stop an oily shine from developing.

Loose powder provides a translucent, natural-looking matte finish. It sets the foundation, and keeps the color of powder eye shadows and blushes strong.

Compact powder is best used for touch-ups during the day. Because it contains a binding agent, pressed powder goes on heavier than loose. It also has a tendency to streak.

Mineral Makeup Powder: Mineral make-up is not just a face powder for the finish after the foundation. As it contains a larger amount of covering agents, it can replace a liquid foundation. Mineral makeup offers many advantages over the traditional makeup of liquid foundations and face powders. It

Basic Ingredients

Cosmetic powders consist of one or more of the following ingredients:

Talc: Talc is a natural mineral consisting of silicon, oxygen and magnesium. It is an excellent filling agent providing texture and good coverage. It has a good slip and adhesiveness and is able to absorb moisture and stabilize fragrances. Talc has been accused of being able to induce cancer, and therefore abandoned in some products, especially in mineral makeup. All accusations, however, could never be confirmed clinically. As summarized in a recent review article by the Biomedical and Environmental Consultants (*Regul Toxicol Pharmacol.* 2002; 36: 40-50) it was concluded that the argument considering talc a carcinogen lacks convincing scientific evidence. Also the FDA lists talc as a generally safe ingredient for both food and cosmetics.

Titanium Dioxide: Titanium dioxide is a white crystalline powder derived from the naturally occurring mineral Ilmenite. It has outstanding covering properties (better than zinc oxide) and is extremely inert. Since it absorbs UVA and UVB rays, titanium dioxide is also widely used as a sunscreen agent. It is also available as micronized, ultra-fine powder.

Zinc Oxide: Zinc oxide is produced from zinc ore, a naturally occurring mineral. It is a fine amorphous powder with good covering properties. It also has UV absorbing and mild deodorant properties. Zinc oxide is also available as micronized powder.

Kaolin: Kaolin is a natural mineral derived from kaolinite (aluminum silicate). It has good covering ability, absorbs oil from the skin, refines pores, and helps clear up breakouts. It also has soothing properties that make it an ideal ingredient for sensitive skin.

Metallic Stearates: One of the most widely used metallic stearates is magnesium stearate. It is a fine, soapy powder made of magnesium and stearic acid. Magnesium stearate is added to improve slip and the adhesiveness of the powder to the skin. It also makes powders more water-resistant.

Corn Starch: Corn starch is widely used in cosmetic powders to increase the flow and to give a "peach-like" bloom to the skin. Corn starch absorbs oils from the skin and is thus often used in "oil-control" products.

Mineral Makeup

Mineral makeup has become a huge trend in the cosmetic industry, with a rapidly growing number of competing products. There is no clear definition what a product must or must not contain to claim to be a mineral makeup. It is widely agreed that the term mineral makeup relates to a kind of makeup that is "powdery" rather than liquid or creamy and contains various mineral powders including sunscreen minerals and pigment minerals, but typically no oily or liquid ingredients.

The Ingredients: Typically, there are the two sunscreen minerals like titanium dioxide and zinc oxide. Often they are used in their micronized, superfine form. Both titanium dioxide and zinc oxide protect the skin from the damaging effects of UVA and UVB sunrays. Since both minerals are white powders, they provide coverage and also help to lighten up the makeup.

The pigments typically include iron oxides and micas. Iron oxides are inorganic, naturally derived mineral pigments typically obtained from china clay or carbon deposits. Micas are also naturally derived pigments and provide shimmer with a smooth and silky feel. Sometimes, bismuth oxychloride is also added to mineral makeup products. Bismuth oxychloride is a pearlescent pigment derived from metallic element bismuth. It provides whiteness, luster and a compact, smooth texture.

In most mineral makeup products, oily ingredients are not included in order to keep the powder very finely ground, light, and easy to apply. The minerals work with the skin's own fatty components to create a smooth cover without looking thick, cakey or dull. Sometimes, however, a small amount of oil is necessary for blending the pigments and keeping them together better.

Often, talc is omitted in mineral makeup, although it is also a naturally derived mineral. As mentioned above, talc has been accused of being able to induce lung cancer upon inhalation. However, this could never be substantiated in clinical trials and many leading cosmetic manufacturer have re-introduced talc in cosmetic products. We think that talc can be used safely in mineral makeup and provide more stability and texture to the powder. Talc may also be especially useful for oily skin.

As mineral makeup does not usually contain water, growth of bacteria is limited and preservatives may be omitted. Zinc oxide may also help to reduce growth of bacteria.

Ingredients for Mineral Makeup
Titanium Dioxide (sunscreen mineral)
Zinc Oxide (sunscreen mineral)
Iron Oxides (pigment minerals)
Micas (glitter pigment minerals)
Bismuth Oxychloride (texturizer
& pigment mineral)

Application: Mineral makeup has several great advantages over traditional liquid foundations. First, mineral makeup provides sun protection, and thus reduces the risk of UV-induced skin aging. It also gives great coverage and looks more like "real skin" than other makeup, as it does not give a mask-like look and feel. Mineral makeup is water resistant and adheres all day long.

Another great advantage is that mineral makeup can be multifunctional products as they combine foundation, sunscreen, makeup and concealer in one. Most women do not need a moisturizer underneath. Mineral makeup is also favorable for those who have allergies or problematic skin such as eczema, acne or other irritations.

Mineral makeup is also very easy and quick to apply. The foundation brush (kabuki brush) gives a smooth "airbrushed" effect and well-controlled coverage around the eyes, nose and lips.

Formulation of Powders

Although makeup powders contain the same basic ingredients, their proportions vary considerably and determine the specific properties of the different powders. The table below shows approximate proportions of basic ingredients in three different makeup powders (numbers indicate percentages). Of course, there is still much variation possible, and additional ingredients can be added.

Ingredient	Transparent Powder	Shimmering Powder	Mineral Makeup
Talc	85-95	20-50	0-5
Tit. Dioxide	0-1	1-5	15-25
Zinc Oxide	0-1	0-1	15-25
Mg. Stearate	5-10	5-10	5-10
Bismuth Oxy.	0-1	5-10	0-15
Kaolin	0-1	0-1	0-1
Iron Oxides	0-5	0-5	10-20
Micas	0-5	50-80	20-50

Loose Mineral Face Powder (I)
Color: Bare Beige, 100 g / 3.6 oz

Light coverage face powder that is applied over foundation or for touch-up during the day. Ideal for those with oily skin or prefer a lighter powder. Can also be used as a body powder.

Method: Add phase A into a mortar and blend well with the pestle until the color is uniform. Test on white paper for color streaking; when uniform add phase B one by one and stir between additions. Fill into jars.

Phase A
Titanium Dioxide 2% (2g / 1/2tsp)
Zinc Oxide 8% (8g / 2tsp + 1/4tsp)
Pigment Blend Bare Beige 6% (6g / 2 1/4tsp)

Phase B
Magnesium Stearate 7% (7g / 1Tbsp + 1/2tsp)
Talc 59.8% (59.8g / 7 1/2Tbsp)
Mica Powder 16% (16g / 5Tbsp + 1tsp)
Fragrance (optional) 0.2% (0.2ml / 5 drops)
Phenoxyethanol-SA (optional) 1% (1ml / 24 drops)

Loose Mineral Face Powder (II)

Color: Bare Neutral, 100 g / 3.6 oz

Medium coverage face powder that is applied over foundation or as a light foundation powder itself on "make-up free" days.

Method: Add phase A into a mortar and blend well with the pestle until the color is uniform. Test on white paper for color streaking. When uniform add phase B one by one and stir between additions. Fill into jars.

Phase A
Titanium Dioxide 4% (4g / 1 1/4tsp)
Zinc Oxide 11% (11g / 1Tbsp)
Pigment Blend Bare Neutral 6% (6g / 2 1/4tsp)

Phase B
Talc 54.8% (54.8 g / 6 3/4Tbsp)
Magnesium Stearate 7% (7g / 1Tbsp + 1/2tsp)
Mica Powder 16% (16g / 5Tbsp + 1tsp)
Fragrance (optional) 0.2% (0.2ml / 5 drops)
Phenoxyethanol-SA (optional) 1% (1ml / 24 drops

Loose Mineral Face Powder with Kaolin
Light Coverage, 100 g / 3.6 oz

Face powder that contains kaolin as oil-absorbing ingredient. Ideal for the skin that tends to shine, oily skin or an oily t-zone.

Method: Add phase A into a mortar and blend well with the pestle until the color is uniform. Test on white paper for color streaking. When uniform add phase B one by one and stir between additions. Fill into powder sifter jars. Color can be adjusted by adding more of the pigment blend to the powder, blend well with mortar and pestle. Kaolin containing products tend to grow molds, especially if they are stored in moist conditions; we therefore recommend preservation.

Phase A
Pigment Blend of your choice 4% (4g / 2tsp)

Titanium Dioxide 8% (8g / 3/4Tbsp)

Phase B
Talc 71.8% (71.8g / 9Tbsp)

Magnesium Stearate 5% (5g / 2 1/2tsp)

Kaolin 10% (10g / 1 3/4Tbsp)

Fragrance (optional) 0.2% (0.2ml / 5 drops)

Phenoxyethanol-SA 1% (1ml / 24 drops)

Wet and Dry Pressed Powder
Color: Pale Beige, 100 g / 3.6 oz

This type of pressed powder (cake make-up) can be applied to the skin with a damp or dry applicator or just with the fingers. It has an extremely velvet feel and creates a smooth, flawless finish.

Method: Add phase A into a mortar and blend well with the pestle until the color is uniform. Test on white paper for color streaking. When uniform add phase B to the mortar and blend again well. Add phase C to phase A/B in the mortar and blend well with the pestle until the color is uniform and the powder is mixed well. Press into jars.

Phase A
Titanium Dioxide 6% (6g / 1 3/4tsp)
Iron Oxide Yellow 1.5% (1.5g / 1tsp)
Iron Oxide Brown 1% (1g / 1/4tsp)
Iron Oxide Red 0.6% (0.6g / 1/8tsp)

Phase B
Talc 55.7% (55.7g / 7 Tbsp)
Mica Powder 20% (20g / 6 3/4Tbsp)
Mica Spheres 8% (8g / 2Tbsp)

Phase C
Polyisobutene-250 4% (4ml / 1tsp)
Triglyceride 2% (2ml / 1/2tsp)
Fragrance (optional) 0.2% (0.2g / 5 drops)
Phenoxyethanol-SA 1% (1ml / 24 drops)

Creamy Powder (I)

Color: Bronze-Tan, 100 g / 3.6 oz

This type of powder needs to be heated and then filled hot into pots or compacts. It applies like a cream but has a powder finish. Triglyceride is a very good pigment dispersant. Avocado butter serves as moisturizer.

Method: Add phase A into a mortar and blend well with the pestle until the color is uniform. Test on white paper for color streaking, and adjust color if necessary. Transfer phase A into a heat resistant glass beaker. Add phase B to phase A in the beaker and stir. Heat phase A/B to 185°F/85°C to melt the waxes, stir until uniform. Remove from heat and add phase C, stir well and fill while still hot into jars or compact containers. The thickness of the product can be adjusted by increasing or reducing the amount of waxes.

Phase A
Titanium Dioxide 2% (2g / 1 3/4tsp)
Iron Oxide Yellow 1.6% (1.6g / 1tsp)
Iron Oxide Red 0.5% (0.5g / 1/8tsp)
Iron Oxide Dark Brown 0.5% (0.5g / 1/8tsp)
Iron Oxide Black 0.2% (0.2g / 1/16tsp)
Isoeicosane 16% (16ml / 1Tbsp + 1/4tsp)

Phase B
Triglyceride 26.5% (26.5ml / 5 1/2tsp)
Avocado Butter 2% (2g / 1/2tsp)
Mica Spheres 16% (16g / 4Tbsp)
Mica Powder 15% (15g / 5Tbsp)
Corn Starch AS 12.5% (12.5g / 1Tbsp + 1/2tsp)
Beeswax 2% (2g / 1tsp)
Carnauba Wax 2% (2g / 1tsp)

Polyglyceryl Oleate 0.5% (0.5g / 12 drops)
Vitamin C L-Ascorbyl Palmitate
   0.5% (0.5g / 12 drops)
Vitamin E Acetate 1% (1ml / 1/4tsp)

Phase C
Vitamin E Tocopherol 0.2% (0.2ml / 5 drops)
Phenoxyethanol-SA 1% (1ml / 24 drops)

Creamy Powder (II)
Color: Light Bisque, 100 g / 3.6 oz

This type of powder needs to be heated then filled hot into pots or compacts. It applies like a cream but has a powder finish. It is formulated with iron oxide pigments that are dispersed in castor oil. Spherical mica helps diminish the appearance of fine lines and wrinkles. The formula contains vitamin C and vitamin E as antioxidants.

Method: Add phase A into a mortar and blend well with the pestle until the color is uniform. Test on white paper for color streaking, and adjust color if necessary. Transfer phase A into a heat resistant glass beaker. Add phase B to phase A in the beaker and stir. Heat phase A/B to 185°F/85°C to melt the waxes, stir until uniform. Remove from heat and add phase C, stir well and fill while still hot into jars or compact containers. The thickness of the product can be adjusted by increasing or reducing the amount of waxes.

Phase A
Titanium Dioxide 5% (5g / 1 1/2tsp)
Isoeicosane 16% (16ml / 1Tbsp + 1/4tsp)
Iron Oxide Brown Dispersion
  0.3% (0.3ml / 7 drops)

Phase B
Triglyceride 26% (26ml / 5 1/2tsp)
Sheabutter 2% (2g / 1/2tsp)
Mica Spheres 16% (16g / 4Tbsp)
Mica Powder 15% (15g / 5Tbsp)
Corn Starch AS 12.5% (12.5g / 1Tbsp + 1/2tsp)
Beeswax 2% (2g / 1tsp)
Carnauba Wax 2% (2g / 1tsp)

Polyglyceryl Oleate 0.5% (0.5g / 12 drops)
Vitamin C L-Ascorbyl Palmitate
  0.5% (0.5g / 12 drops)
Vitamin E Acetate 1% (1ml / 1/4tsp)

Phase C
Vitamin E Tocopherol 0.2% (0.2ml / 5 drops)
Phenoxyethanol-SA 1% (1ml / 24 drops)

Creamy Powder (III)

Color: Sunny Beige, Light Skin, 100 g / 3.6 oz

This type of powder needs to be heated then filled hot into pots or compacts. It applies like a cream but has a powder finish. This formula is softer than the previous ones and it additionally contains a fragrance. The spherical mica helps diminish the appearance of fine lines and wrinkles.

Method: Add phase A into a mortar and blend well with the pestle until the color is uniform. Test on white paper for color streaking, and if uniform add phase B to the mortar. Wet and blend the pigments well until the color is uniform. Transfer phase A/B into a heat resistant glass beaker. Add phase C to phase A/B in the beaker and heat to 160°F/71°C to melt the wax, stir well until uniform. Add phase D to phase A/B and stir again then remove from heat and fill into jars or compact containers. The thickness of the product can be adjusted by increasing or reducing the amount of waxes.

Phase A
Titanium Dioxide 7% (7g / 2tsp)
Iron Oxide Yellow 0.8% (0.8g / 1/2tsp)
Iron Oxide Red 0.2% (0.2g / 1/16tsp)
Iron Oxide Black 0.1% (0.1g / <1/16tsp)

Phase B
Meadowfoam Seed Oil 15% (15ml / 1Tbsp)

Phase C
Polyisobutene-800 18% (18ml / 1Tbsp + 1/2tsp)
Triglyceride 15% (15ml / 1Tbsp)
Mica Powder 12.5% (12.5g / 4Tbsp)
Mica Spheres 10% (10g / 2 1/2Tbsp)

Corn Starch AS 13% (13g / 1Tbsp + 1tsp)
Mycrocrystalline Wax 7% (7g / 1Tbsp)
Polyglyceryl Oleate 0.5% (0.5ml / 12 drops)
BHT 0.2% (0.2g / 1/16tsp)

Phase D
Fragrance 0.2% (0.2ml / 5 drops)
Paraben-DU 0.5% (0.5ml / 12 drops)

Basic Velvet Mineral Makeup Powder
Color: Bare Neutral or "Your Choice", 50 g / 1.8 oz

This is a loose mineral makeup made with a premixed pigment blend of a natural skin color (bare neutral) for easy formulating. The shades, however, can still be adjusted with titanium dioxide. High sun protection, easy application and a flawless natural look make this kind of makeup so trendy. Spherical mica has been added to help diminish the appearance of fine lines and wrinkles.

Method: Add phase A into a mortar and blend well with the pestle until the color is uniform. Test on white paper for color streaking, and if uniform place in a separate dish. Add phase B to the mortar and blend well with the pestle until uniform, remove from the mortar. Add phase A back to the mortar and add phase B until the color matches your skin tone, blend well with the pestle between steps until the color is uniform. Then add phase C and stir again well. Fill into powder sifter jars.

Phase A
Titanium Dioxide 5% (2.5g / 3/4tsp)

Pigment Blend Bare Neutral or
   one of your choice 17% (8.5g / 1Tbsp)

Phase B
Mica Powder 39.8% (19.9g / 6 3/4Tbsp)

Micronized Zinc Oxide 15% (7.5g / 1Tbsp + 3/4tsp)

Mica Spheres 20% (10g / 2 1/2Tbsp)

Phase C
Fragrance (optional) 0.2% (0.1ml / 2 drops)

Phenoxyethanol-SA (optional) 1% (0.5ml / 12 drops)

Sheer Mineral Makeup Powder
Color: Warm Beige, 30 g / 1.0 oz

This recipe gives a loose mineral makeup. It is made not by a premixed pigment blend but different iron oxide pigments which let you create your very own shade (amounts in recipe gives a warm beige shade). Pearlwhite and gold mica create a healthy glow. Fine lines and wrinkles are diminished with spherical mica. This powder makeup adheres very well to the skin and gives a flawless natural look.

Method: Add phase A into a mortar and blend well with the pestle until the color is uniform. Test on white paper for color streaking, and if uniform, add phase B one by one and blend well during each addition with the pestle. The color can be adjusted by adding more pigments for a more intense color, or mica powder to dilute too much color. Ultramarine blue has been added to control the red color. Fill into powder sifter jars.

Phase A
Iron Oxide Yellow 3% (0.9g / 1/2tsp)
Iron Oxide Red 1.5% (0.45g / 1/4tsp)
Iron Oxide Black 0.5% (0.15g / 1/8tsp)
Ultramarine Blue 0.1% (0.03g / <1/16tsp)
Titanium Dioxide 8% (2.4g / 3/4tsp)

Phase B
Micronized Zinc Oxide 14% (4.2g / 2tsp)
Mica Powder 50.1% (15g / 5Tbsp)
Mica Spheres 19.8% (5.9g / 1 1/2Tbsp)
Mica Pearlwhite 1% (0.3g / 1/8tsp)
Mica Gold 1% (0.3g / 1/8tsp)
Phenoxyethanol-SA (optional) 1% (0.3g / 7 drops)

Velvet Mineral Makeup Powder
Color: Chestnut Brown, 30 g / 1.0 oz

As the recipe on page 79, this is a loose mineral makeup made with a premixed pigment blend of a natural skin color (chestnut brown) for easy formulating. Spherical mica help reduce fine lines and wrinkles for a flawless natural look.

Method: Add phase A into a mortar and blend well with the pestle until the color is uniform. Test on white paper for color streaking, and if uniform add phase B one by one and blend well with the pestle during each addition. The color can be adjusted by adding more of the pigment blends for a more intense color, or mica powder to dilute too much color. Fill into powder sifter jars.

Phase A
Pigment Blend Dark Brown 28% (8.4g / 1Tbsp)
Pigment Blend Caramel 12% (3.6g / 1 3/4tsp)
Micronized Zinc Oxide 5% (1.5g / 1tsp)

Phase B
Mica Powder 41.6% (12.5g / 4Tbsp)
Mica Spheres 12% (3.6g / 1Tbsp)
Phenoxyethanol-SA (optional) 1% (0.3ml / 7 drops)

Sheer Mineral Veil

Color: Bare Beige, 30 g / 1.0 oz

This sheer powder is oil-absorbing, sets and perfects color to create a smooth, silky finish. Add spherical mica, a light diffusing pigment, to diminish the appearance of fine lines and wrinkles. Kaolin provides effective oil control.

Method: Add phase A into a mortar and blend well with the pestle until the color is uniform. Test on white paper for color streaking, and when uniform add phase B one by one and blend well after each addition with the pestle. Add phase C at last and stir again well with the pestle. The color can be adjusted by adding more of the pigment blends for a more intense color, or mica powder to dilute too much color. Fill into powder sifter jars.

Phase A
Pigment Blend Bare Beige 8% (2.4g / 1tsp)
Micronized Zinc Oxide 8% (2.4g / 1 1/4tsp)

Phase B
Mica Powder 47% (14.1 / 4Tbsp + 2tsp)
Mica Spheres 23% (6.9g / 1 3/4Tbsp)
Corn Starch AS 5% (1.5g / 3/4tsp)
Magnesium Stearate 5% (1.5g / 3/4tsp)
Kaolin 3% (0.9g / 1/2tsp)

Phase C
Phenoxyethanol-SA (optional) 1% (0.3ml / 7 drops)

Touch-Up Veil
Color: Bare Neutral, 50 g / 1.8 oz

This recipe gives a silky transparent veil to use over foundation as a finishing touch or for easy touch-ups during the day. Cornstarch controls oil and the spherical mica minimizes fine lines and wrinkles.

Method: Add phase A into a mortar and blend well with the pestle until the color is uniform. Test on white paper for color streaking, and when uniform add phase B one by one and blend well with the pestle after each addition. Add phase C at last and stir again well with the pestle. The color can be adjusted by adding more of the pigment blend for a more intense color, or mica spheres to dilute too much color. Fill into powder sifter jars.

Phase A
Pigment Blend Bare Neutral 8% (4g / 1/2Tbsp)
Magnesium Stearate 7% (3.5g / 1 3/4tsp)

Phase B
Corn Starch AS 68% (34g / 3Tbsp + 2tsp)
Mica Spheres 16% (8g / 2Tbsp)

Phase C
Phenoxyethanol-SA (optional) 1% (0.5ml / 12 drops)

Mineral Bronzing Powder
Color: Medium Tan, 50 g / 1.8 oz

This formula gives a pleasant mineral bronzing powder that provides your skin the look of a natural tan for a nice, healthy sun-kissed look. Contains corn starch for effective oil control.

Method: Add phase A into a mortar and blend well with the pestle until the color is uniform. Test on white paper for color streaking, and when uniform add phase B one by one and blend after each addition with the pestle. Add phase C at last and stir again well. The color can be adjusted by adding more of the iron oxide or mica pigments for a more intense color, or mica powder to dilute too much color. Fill into powder sifter jars.

Phase A
Micronized Zinc Oxide 5% (2.5g / 1 1/4tsp)
Iron Oxide Red 2% (1g / 1/4tsp)
Iron Oxide Brown 4% (2g / 1/2tsp)
Iron Oxide Yellow 3.5% (1.8g / 1tsp)
Iron Oxide Black 1% (0.5g / 1/8-1/4tsp)
Magnesium Stearate 6% (3g / 1 1/2tsp)

Phase B
Mica Powder 30% (15g / 5Tbsp)
Corn Starch AS 24.3% (12.2g / 1Tbsp + 1/2tsp)
Mica Spheres 20% (10g / 2 1/2Tbsp)
Mica Gold 1.5% (0.75g / 1/4-1/2tsp)
Mica Bronze 1.5% (0.75g / 1/4-1/2tsp)

Phase C
Fragrance (optional) 0.2% (0.1ml / 2 drops)
Phenoxyethanol-SA (optional) 1% (0.5ml / 12 drops)

Solid Bronzing Stick
Color: Warm Bronze, 50 g / 1.8 oz

A bronzing color adds a healthy glow to any complexion and instantly gives your skin the look of a natural tan. Use on cheeks, nose and forehead where the sun would naturally hit, for a healthy glow. Contains a sun protection factor of 8-12 together with antioxidants such as vitamin C and vitamin E. Sheabutter is added for a good moisturizing effect.

Method: Add phase A into a heat resistant glass beaker and heat to 176°F/80°C to melt the wax. Add phase B to phase A and stir until uniform. Remove from heat. Add phase C to phase A/B and fill into stick tubes, pots or mold.

Phase A
Beeswax 8% (4g / 2tsp)
Carnauba Wax 4% (2g / 1tsp)
Macadamia Nut Oil 10% (5ml / 1tsp)
Sheabutter 8% (4g / 1tsp)
Triglyceride 34.5% (17.3ml / 1Tbsp + 1/2tsp)
OM-Cinnamate 6% (3ml / 1/2tsp)
Polyglyceryl Oleate 0.5% (0.25ml / 6 drops)
Iron Oxide Color Dispersion 2% (1ml / 1/4tsp)
Vitamin C L-Ascorbyl Palmitate 0.5% (0.25g / 1/8tsp)

Phase B
Mica Spheres 8.8% (4.4g / 1Tbsp + 1/4tsp)
Corn Starch AS 8% (4g / 1 1/4tsp)
Mica Gold 7% (3.5g / 1 3/4tsp)
Mica Bronze 2% (1g / 1/2tsp)

Phase C
Vitamin E Tocopherol 0.2% (0.1ml / 2 drops)
Phenoxyethanol-SA 1% (0.5ml / 12 drops)

Blush Makeup

Introduction

Blushers are designed to give your skin a glowing, radiant and fresh look. They are available in powder, gel or solid form, and in a wide variety of tones. Powders give a nice matte finish, and are long-lasting in wear. If powders, however, are not properly formulated, they can crumble, and the color can become too intense when applied over a creamy foundation.

Ingredients

Mica: Micas are magnesium aluminum silicates, a natural mineral. Depending on their particle size and coating with additional color minerals, micas can add transparency to a product or also shimmering or pearlizing effects in various colors.

Colors: Colors used in blushes include both inorganic (pigments) and organic colors (dyes and lakes). All FDA approved dyes are acceptable for blushers. Formulating with mica pigments, however, is often easier because their color intensity is lower. For deep and more intense red shades dyes and lakes (e.g. D&C red no. 6 or 7) are used, typically at a concentration of 0.5-2%.

Spherical Ingredients: To obtain a soft and matte finish of the blush, tiny spherical ingredients such as mica spheres are often used. Such beads are able to scatter light in different directions, making the skin appear soft and blurred. Small wrinkles also become invisible. This effect is called "soft-focus".

Magnesium Stearate: Magnesium stearate is a fine white soapy powder ideal to give blushes adhesiveness and texture.

Corn Starch, Kaolin, and Talc: see page 69 and 70 for detailed description.

Formulation

Powder Blush: Typically, blush powders consist of two phases, the oil phase and the dry phase. The oil phase contains natural or synthetic oils, which wet the pigments to fully develop their colors. Oils are also important for making pressed powders, as they help to form a "cake" and hold the powders together. The dry phase contains the pigments and filling agents like talc and magnesium stearate.

For making pressed powder blushes, you don't need a cosmetic powder press. You can find a suitable tool at a hardwood store.

Gel Blush: Gel blushers contain special oily components that are volatile, allowing the blush to dry after it is applied to the skin. The most widely used components are special hydrocarbons like isoeicosane or natural oils which are absorbed by the skin. Gel blushes can be formulated with or without water.

Solid Blush/Blush Stick: Solid blushes are formulated similar to gel blushes but contain a harder wax. Blush sticks contain more waxes for stability.

Pressed Blush Powder (I)

Color: Tawny, 30 g / 1.0 oz

Pressed blush powder with colored mica which give a fresh and natural look. Peony is a beautiful shade for a "pop of color" over your regular blush shade.

Method: Add phase A into a mortar and blend well with the pestle until the color is uniform and does not show color streaking.

Add phase B to phase A and stir very well. Add phase C to phase A/B and blend again well with the pestle until uniform. If necessary adjust the color with micas colors for a more intense shade, or dilute the color with mica powder or talc for a less intense color. Press into blush pots.

Phase A
Titanium Dioxide 3% (0.9g / 1/4tsp)
Mica Bordeaux 2% (0.6g / 1/4tsp)
Mica Pearlwhite 6% (1.8g / 3/4tsp)
Mica Oriental Beige 1% (0.3g / 1/8tsp)
D&C Red-6 0.5% (0.15g / 1/16tsp)

Phase B
Cyclo-Dimethicone 5% (1.5g / 36 drops)
Polyglyceryl Oleate 0.5% (0.25g / 5 drops)

Phase C
Talc 53% (15.8g / 1Tbsp)
Mica Powder 24% (7.2g / 2Tbsp + 1tsp)
Magnesium Stearate 5% (1.5g / 3/4tsp)

Pressed Blush Powder (II)

Color: Desert Flower, 30 g / 1.0 oz

Pressed blush powder with mica pigments for a hue of bronze and red for colors that looks rich and natural. Talc works very well for making pressed blushes because it has optimum compression qualities.

Method: Add phase A into a mortar and blend well with the pestle until the color is uniform and does not show streaking. Add phase B to phase A and again stir very well with the pestle. Test the color on white paper. The color is good when there is no streaking. Add phase C to phase A/B and stir well. If necessary adjust the color with mica colors for a more intense color, or dilute the color with mica powder or talc for a less intense color. Press into blush pots.

Phase A
Mica Bronze 1% (0.3g / 1/8tsp)
Mica Bordeaux 9% (2.7g / 1 1/2tsp)
Mica Pearlwhite 4% (1.2g / 1/2tsp)
Zinc Oxide 2% (0.6g / 1/4tsp)

Phase B
Jojoba Oil 2% (0.6ml / 14 drops)
Cyclo-Dimethicone 4% (1.2ml / 30 drops)
Polyglyceryl Oleate 0.5% (0.15ml / 5 drops)

Phase C
Talc 54.5% (16.4 g / 2Tbsp)
Mica Powder 18% (5.4g / 1 3/4Tbsp)
Magnesium Stearate 5% (1.5g / 3/4tsp)

Loose Blush Powder (I)
Color: Pale Pink, 30 g / 1.0 oz

Powder blush with carmine and pearl white mica for a light pink shade, formulated with corn starch and kaolin as oil absorbers. Pale pink is a beautiful shade for a 'pop of color' over your regular blush shade.

Method: Add phase A into a mortar and blend well with the pestle until the color is uniform. Test on white paper for color streaking. Then add phase B to phase A and mix well with the pestle until uniform. Finally add phase C and stir. If necessary adjust the color with mica colors for a more intense color, or dilute the color with mica spheres or talc for a less intense color. Add to a small powder shaker jar.

Phase A
Kaolin 5% (1.5g / 3/4tsp)
Magnesium Stearate 5% (1.5g / 3/4tsp)
Titanium Dioxide 2% (0.6g / 1/4tsp)
Mica Carmine Red 4% (1.2g / 1/2tsp)
Mica Pearlwhite 6% (1.8g / 3/4tsp)

Phase B
Mica Spheres 15% (4.5g / 1Tbsp)
Talc 45% (13.5g / 1 1/2Tbsp)
Corn Starch AS 15% (4.5g / 1/2Tbsp)

Phase C
Pearlwhite Mica 3% (0.9g / 1/2tsp)

Loose Blush Powder (II)

Color: Mauve, 30 g / 1.0 oz

Loose blush powder with mauve color which gives a fresh and natural look. This silky formula glides on very smoothly. As mentioned in previous blush powder recipes, you can create many different shades by adding more of the mica colors for a more intense color or more of the mica powder for a less intense color. The combinations are endless.

Method: Add phase A into a mortar and blend well with the pestle until the color is uniform. Test on white paper for color streaking. Add phase B to phase A and blend well until uniform. Finally add phase C and stir. Add to a small powder shaker jar.

Phase A
Mica Pearlwhite 3% (0.9g / 1/2tsp)

Mica Red 3% (0.9g / 1/2tsp)

Mica Blackstar Red 2% (0.6g / 1/4tsp)

Titanium Dioxide 2% (0.6g / 1/4tsp)

Ultramarine Pink 4% (1.2g / 1/2tsp)

Phase B
Mica Powder 50% (15g / 5Tbsp)

Mica Spheres 29% (8.7g / 2Tbsp)

Magnesium Stearate 5% (1.5g / 3/4tsp)

Phase C
Mica Pearlwhite 2% (0.6g / 1/4tsp)

Aqueous Gel Blush

Color: Sand Pink, 30 g / 1.0 oz

Nicely moisturizing gel blush that contains water. It is non-oily and dries quickly. Provitamin B5 moisturizes and soothes the skin. Ideal for dry and brittle skin or as a soothing agent after a day in the sun.

Method: This recipe does not require heating. Add phase A into a glass beaker and stir well. Add phase B to another glass beaker and mix the ingredients until uniform. Add phase C to a mortar and blend until uniform, then add to phase A and stir. Add phase B to phase A/C and stir very well with a little hand mixer until thick and uniform. The thickness of the gel can be adjusted with GelMaker EMU. Fill into containers.

Phase A
Distilled Water 66.5% (20ml / 4tsp)

Corn Starch AS 4% (1.2g / 1/2tsp)

Glycerin 2% (0.6ml / 14 drops)

Phase B
Triglyceride 8% (2.4ml / 1/2tsp)

GelMaker EMU 3.5% (1.1ml / 24 drops)

Provitamin B5 0.5% (0.15g / 4 drops)

Phase C
Mica Carmine Red 4% (1.2g / 1/2tsp)

Mica Blackstar Red 2% (0.6g / 1/4tsp)

Mica Pearlwhite 6% (1.8g / 1 3/4tsp)

Mica Gold 2% (0.6g / 1/4tsp)

Phenoxyethanol-SA 1.5% (0.5ml / 12 drops)

Water-Free Gel Blush (I)
Color: Peony, 30 g / 1.0 oz

Creamy blush to blot on cheeks or lips for a sheer, stained finish. The formula gives a soft viscous gel that does not contain any water, but only pigments and various emollients including avocado butter. Mica spheres give a velvet feel.

Method: Add phase B into a mortar and blend well with the pestle until uniform. Test on white paper for color streaking. Add phase A to a heat resistant glass beaker and heat to 165°F/74°C to melt the wax, stir well. Add phase B to phase A and stir well until the color is uniform. The color can be adjusted by adding more of the mica pigments or D&C red for a more intense color or more mica spheres for a less intense color. Remove the beaker from the heat then add phase C to phase A/B, stir and fill into blush containers.

Phase A
Macadamia Nut Oil 25% (7.5ml / 1 1/2tsp)
Triglyceride 30% (9ml / 2tsp)
Microcrystalline Wax 5% (1.5g / 1/2tsp)
Avocado Butter 3% (0.9g / 1/4tsp)
Polyglyceryl Oleate 1% (0.3ml / 8 drops)
D&C Red No. 7 Dispersion 0.5% (0.15ml / 4 drops)

Phase B
Titanium Dioxide 2% (0.9g / 1/4tsp)
Ultramarine Pink 4% (1.2g / 1/2tsp)
Mica Bordeaux 2% (0.6g / 1/4tsp)
Mica Pearlwhite 6% (1.8g / 1tsp)
Mica Spheres 12.3% (3.7g / 1Tbsp)
Corn Starch AS 8% (2.4g / 3/4tsp)

Phase C
Vitamin E Tocopherol 0.2% (0.06ml / 1 drop)
Phenoxyethanol-SA 1% (0.3ml / 7 drops)

Water-Free Gel Blush (II)
Color: Oriental Rose, 30 g / 1.0 oz

This recipe is similar as the previous one but contains more moisturizing emollients as isoeicosane. This blush is therefore especially suited for dry skin. The texture is creamy viscous and the color quite transparent. Blot on cheeks or lips for a sheer, stained finish.

Method: Add phase B into a mortar and blend well with the pestle until uniform. Test on white paper for color streaking. Add phase A to a heat resistant glass beaker and heat to 165°F/74°C to melt the wax, stir well. Add phase B to phase A and stir well until the color is uniform. The color can be adjusted by adding more of the mica pigments for a more intense color or more mica spheres for a less intense color. Remove the beaker from the heat then add phase C to phase A/B, stir and fill while still hot into blush containers.

Phase A
Meadowfoam Seed Oil 22.8% (6.8ml / 1 1/2tsp)
Isoeicosane 8% (2.4g / 1/2tsp)
Triglyceride 24% (7.2ml / 1 1/2tsp)
Microcrystalline Wax 5% (1.5g / 1/2 - 3/4tsp)
Sheabutter 3% (0.9g / 1/4tsp)
Polyglyceryl Oleate 1% (0.3ml / 8 drops)

Phase B
Titanium Dioxide 2% (0.6g / 1/4tsp)
Mica Oriental Beige 2% (0.6g / 1/4tsp)
Mica Bordeaux 9% (2.7g / 1 1/2tsp)
Mica Spheres 18% (5.4g / 1Tbsp + 1tsp)
Corn Starch AS 4% (1.2g / 1/2tsp)

Phase C
Vitamin E Tocopherol 0.2% (0.06ml / 1 drop)
Phenoxyethanol-SA 1% (0.3ml / 7 drops)

Solid Pot Blush for Cheeks & Lips (I)
Color: Spice Red, 30 g / 1.0 oz

Create a healthy flush with this sheer, lightweight blush. It is a dual-use formula for both cheeks and lips. Nourishing emollients and two different vitamin E forms are major components in this formula. This blush type is a bit more solid than the gel formulas.

Method: Add phase B into a mortar and blend well with the pestle until uniform. Test on white paper for color streaking. Add phase A into a heat resistant glass beaker and heat to 176°F/80°C to melt the wax. Add phase B to phase A and stir well until the color is uniform. The color can be adjusted by adding more of the mica pigments for a more intense color or more mica powder for a less intense color. Remove from the heat and add phase C, stir and fill while still hot into pots or blush containers.

Phase A
Triglyceride 42% (12.6ml / 2 1/2tsp)
Almond Oil 18% (5.4ml / 1tsp)
Carnauba Wax 4% (1.2g / 1/2tsp)
Avocado Butter 5% (1.5g / 1/2tsp)

Phase B
Talc 10% (3g / 1tsp)
Mica Red 10% (3g / 1 1/2tsp)
Titanium Dioxide 2% (0.6g / 1/4tsp)
Iron Oxide Red 0.5% (0.15g / <1/16tsp)
Mica Powder 6.8% (2g / 3/4Tbsp)

Phase C
Vitamin E Tocopherol 0.2% (0.06ml / 1 drop)
Vitamin E Acetate 0.5% (0.15ml / 5 drops)
Phenoxyethanol-SA 1% (0.3ml / 7 drops)

Solid Pot Blush for Cheeks & Lips (II)

Color: Plum, 30 g / 1.0 oz

Creamy non-oily blush that is absorbed quickly by the skin leaving a semi-matte finish. Sheabutter and meadowfoam seed oil will deeply moisturize keeping your cheeks looking fresh and supple. It is formulated to use also on the lips.

Method: Add phase B into a mortar and blend well with the pestle until the color is uniform. Test on white paper for color streaking. Make color adjustments if necessary. Add phase A into a heat resistant glass beaker and heat to 176°F/80°C to melt the wax. Add phase B to phase A and stir well until the color is uniform. Remove from the heat and add phase C, stir and fill while still hot into pots or blush containers.

Phase A
Triglyceride 44.8% (13.4ml / 2 3/4tsp)
Meadowfoam Seed Oil 15% (4.5ml / 1tsp)
Carnauba Wax 4% (1.2g / 1/2tsp)
Sheabutter 5% (1.5g / 1/2tsp)
D&C Red No. 7 Dispersion 0.5% (0.15ml / 4 drops)

Phase B
Titanium Dioxide 2% (0.6g / 1/4tsp)
Mica Bordeaux 5% (1.5g / 3/4tsp)
Mica Blackstar Red 2% (0.6g / 1/4tsp)
Mica Pearlwhite 6% (1.8g / 1tsp)
Mica Powder 14% (4.2g / 1Tbsp + 1tsp)

Phase C
Vitamin E Tocopherol 0.2% (0.06ml / 1 drop)
Vitamin E Acetate 0.5% (0.15ml / 5 drops)
Phenoxyethanol-SA 1% (0.3ml / 7 drops)

Solid Pot Blush for Cheeks & Lips (III)

Color: Brown Berry, 30 g / 1.0 oz

Solid dual-use pot blush that contains different mica pigments but also a small amount of D&C red pigment as a base color. Cocoa butter gives texture to the blush and moisturizes the skin, so does the jojoba oil and isoeicosane. Isoeicosane is a substitute for mineral oil and has the advantage to give a satin feel to products. Blot on cheeks or lips for a sheer, stained finish.

Method: Add phase B into a mortar and blend well with the pestle until the color is uniform. Test on white paper for color streaking, and make color adjustments if necessary. Add phase A into a heat resistant glass beaker and heat to 176°F/80°C to melt the wax. Add phase B to phase A and stir well until uniform. Remove from the heat and add phase C, stir and fill while still hot into pots or blush containers.

Phase A
Triglyceride 42.8% (14ml / 1Tbsp)
Isoeicosane 10% (3ml / 1/2tsp)
Jojoba Oil 10% (3ml / 1/2tsp)
Carnauba Wax 4% (1.2g / 1/2tsp)
Cocoa Butter 3% (0.9g / 1/2tsp)
D&C Red No. 7 Dispersion 0.5% (0.15ml / 4 drops)

Phase B
Titanium Dioxide 2% (0.6g / 1/4tsp)
Mica Bordeaux 5% (1.5g / 3/4tsp)
Mica Blackstar Red 1% (0.3g / 1/8tsp)
Mica Carmine Red 4% (1.2g / 1/2tsp)
Mica Pearlwhite 4% (1.2g / 1/2tsp)
Talc 12% (3.6g / 1 1/2tsp)

Phase C
Vitamin E Tocopherol 0.2% (0.06ml / 1 drop)
Vitamin E Acetate 0.5% (0.15ml / 5 drops)
Phenoxyethanol-SA 1% (0.3ml / 7 drops)

Blush Stick (I)

Color: Spice, 50 g / 1.8 oz

Add a dewy glow to dry skin with this rich sheabutter blush. Formulated with the antioxidants vitamin E and vitamin C to protect the skin from environmental stress.

Method: Add phase B into a mortar and blend well with the pestle until the color is uniform. Test on white paper for color streaking, and make color adjustments if necessary. Add phase A into a heat resistant glass beaker and heat to 176°F/80°C to melt the ingredients. Add phase B to phase A and stir until uniform. Remove from the heat and add phase C. Stir and fill while still hot into blush stick containers or big lip balm tubes.

Phase A
Sheabutter 15% (7.5g / 2tsp)

Isoeicosane 6% (3ml / 1/2tsp)

Triglyceride 20% (10ml / 2tsp)

Meadowfoam Seed Oil 17.3% (8.7ml / 1/2Tbsp)

Ozokerite Wax 10% (5g / 2tsp)

Corn Starch AS 6% (3g / 1tsp)

Candelilla Wax 4% (2g / 3/4tsp)

Vitamin E Acetate 1% (0.5ml / 12 drops)

Vitamin C L-Ascorbyl Palmitate 0.5% (0.25g / 1/8tsp)

Phase B
Titanium Dioxide 2% (1g / 1/4tsp)

Mica Pearlwhite 6% (3g / 1 1/2 tsp)

Mica Gold 5% (2.5g / 1 1/4tsp)

Mica Bordeaux 6% (3g / 1 1/2tsp)

Phase C
Vitamin E Tocopherol 0.2% (0.1ml / 2 drops)

Phenoxyethanol-SA 1% (0.5ml / 12 drops)

Blush Stick (II)

Color: Mauve, 50 g / 1.8 oz

Blush stick with softening avocado butter that moisturizes the cheeks. It is perfect for a healthy flush and a look that is fresh, and dewy. Antioxidants such as vitamin E and vitamin A palmitate protect the skin from environmental stress.

Method: Add phase B into a mortar and blend well with the pestle until the color is uniform. Test on white paper for color streaking. Add phase A into a heat resistant glass beaker and heat to 176°F/80°C to melt the ingredients. Add phase B to phase A and stir until uniform. Remove from the heat and add phase C. Stir and fill while still hot into blush stick containers or big lip balm tubes.

Phase A
Avocado Butter 16% (8g / 2tsp)
Isoeicosane 6% (3ml / 1/2tsp)
Triglyceride 20% (10ml / 2tsp)
Meadowfoam Seed Oil 17.5% (8.8ml / 1/2Tbsp)
Ozokerite Wax 10% (5g / 2tsp)
Corn Starch AS 8% (4g / 1 1/4tsp)
Candelilla Wax 4% (2g / 3/4tsp)
Vitamin E Acetate 1% (0.5ml / 12 drops)
Vitamin A Palmitate 0.3% (0.15ml / 5 drops)

Phase B
Ultramarine Pink 4.5% (2.3g / 1tsp)
Titanium Dioxide 3% (1.5g / 1/2tsp)
Mica Pearlwhite 7% (3.5g / 1 3/4tsp)
Mica Red 2.5% (2.5g / 1 1/4tsp)

Phase C
Vitamin E Tocopherol 0.2% (0.1ml / 2 drops)
Phenoxyethanol-SA 1% (0.5ml / 12 drops)

Lipstick, Lip Gloss & Lip Balm

Introduction

Lipsticks: A good lipstick should meet several criteria: It should apply to the lips easily and evenly without bleeding into the fine lines around the mouth. It should feel moist, not dry, and give good color coverage, yet look natural. Further, a lipstick should have the right consistency, not be too soft or too hard so that it cracks or crumbles during use. A lipstick should also not "sweat" during storage. Lipsticks are basically mixtures of waxes, oils and pigments. By varying the proportions of these ingredients you can determine the characteristics of the final product. For example, a high wax, low oil, and high pigment content results in a long-wearing lipstick with a rather low degree of gloss, texture, and softness. On the other hand, a low wax and high oil content will apply more smoothly, have a greater shine, but will not wear as long.

Lip Gloss: A lip gloss should apply easily and provide a wet, shiny look. It should have a transparent, sheer color coverage and feel moist, pleasant and not tacky on the lips. The fragrance of flavor may be higher than in lipsticks. Like lipsticks, lip glosses consist of a mixture of oils, pigments and waxes. The major difference is that gloss and transparent coverage are the key properties required, and consequently, the oil to wax ratio is higher, and the pigment content is lower than in lipsticks.

Lip Balms: A lipbalm should leave a protective film on the lips that softens and moisturizes the lips. UV protection is optional but a good additive. Lip balms consist of oils, butters and waxes and can be poured directly into lip balm containers and don't require molding. They can also be poured into pots and applied with the fingers.

Ingredients

Lipstick and lip gloss products typically consist of the following ingredients:

Waxes: Waxes form the backbone of lipsticks as they make sure that the sticks become hard and rigid. Most often carnauba wax, candelilla wax, beeswax, ozokerite wax, and microcrystalline wax are utilized.

Carnauba wax is primarily used to provide hardness, rigidity and thermal stability as it has a high melting point of 80-85°C (176-185°F).

Candelilla wax has a lower melting point than carnauba wax (about 69-73°C, 156-163°F), and is therefore less hard and rigid. It provides, however, more shine and is less grainy than carnauba wax.

Beeswax has one of the lowest melting point of natural waxes (about 61-68°C, 142-154°F) and is less hard, but makes the lipstick smooth and pleasant to apply.

Natural mineral waxes like ozokerite wax (melt at 73-76°C, 164-169°F) or micro-crystalline wax (melt at 63-68°C, 145-155°F) are often used to enhance the consistency and hardness of the lipstick. Both waxes are less brittle than carnauba wax and are also useful to ensure color uniformity and avoid sweating.

Oils & Butters: The oil most often used for lipsticks and lip gloss is castor oil. It gives a nice shine, helps to disperse the colors, has acceptable color, odor and taste, and is inexpensive. Typically, castor oil is used between 20-45%. Formulas with more than 50% have limited stability and leave a heavy, greasy feel on the lips with a unpleasant taste. Plant oils like grapeseed oil, almond oil, rose hip oil or meadowfoam seed oil can also be used, but are more expensive. Plant oils need to be combined with antioxidants (e.g. vitamin E or BHT) to prevent them from becoming rancid.

Butters like sheabutter or avocado butter are also useful in lipsticks as they provide similar properties as oils. In some lipstick formulations, fatty acid esters like isopropyl myristate or isopropyl palmitate are added. Such esters have been found to gelatinize waxes and improve the adhesiveness to the lips.

Hydrocarbons: Branched-chain hydrocarbons like isododecane, isoeicosane and polyisobutene are widely used non-wax base materials in lipsticks. These compounds help maintain a porous film on the lips preventing moisture loss. They also provide long lasting wear properties, satiny feel and high sheen to the lips. Hydrocarbons are also suitable substitutes for mineral oil in "oil-free" products.

Colors: Basically, three different types of colorants are used for lipsticks and lip gloss products. These include organic colors, inorganic mineral pigments, and glitter pigments (micas). The organic colors commonly used include D&C Red No. 6, 7, 21, 22, 27, 28, and 30, FD&C yellow No. 5 and 6, D&C orange No. 5, and FD&C blue No. 1. The inorganic pigments include titanium dioxide, and iron oxide yellow, red and black. The most frequently used glitter pigments are micas coated with titanium dioxide. They are available in various colors and particle sizes producing either a fine, transparent luster or large, colored sparkle (see also pages 26-33).

Molding Lipsticks

The method to produce the lipstick mass is described in detail within the recipes. The hot mass will be used immediately to form sticks in a lipstick mold. The most common method for molding lipsticks is by use of vertical split molds. As metal molds used by the cosmetic industry are very expensive, we have designed a special 3-cavity plastic mold that is ideal for home use.

First, grease the mold with oil and pour the hot liquid carefully into the mold. Do not interrupt filling since the lipstick may then consist of different layers and break apart. At the end there may be a little hole on the top. Just top it off. Then put the mold in the refrigerator for half an hour. After the mass has hardened, remove the lipstick from the mold. This is best done by pushing it carefully, and bottom-first out of the cavity. If the lipstick gets a dent after you have pushed it out of the mold, the lipstick may be too soft and require more waxes to make it harder. The lipstick can then be put into the sleeve of the lipstick holder. Cut off the tip obliquely to give the lipstick its typical shape. Finally, you can pass the lipstick through a candle flame, which makes the surface nicely glossy.

Prepare lipstick mass. Grease the mold & close it tightly (possibly with a rubberband).

Pour the still hot lipstick mass (about 70°C/ 160°F) into the mold.

Let the lipsticks harden in the refrigerator for about 30 min. Open the mold carefully.

Remove the lipsticks by pushing them gently out of the cavities bottom-first.

Cut off the tip of the lipstick with a knife to give the lipstick its typical shape.

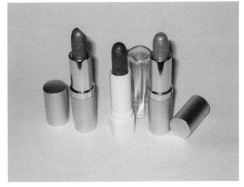

Stick the lipsticks carefully into the sleeves. You may flame the tips to increase its gloss.

Burgundy Red Lipstick
Color: Burgundy, 50 g / 1.8 oz, 8-10 Lipsticks

Creamy, smooth lipstick that gives lips instant polish with rich, full color. Vitamin E and vitamin C act as antioxidants and protect the lips from environmental stress. Contains a natural sun protection factor of 4-6.

Method: Add phase A into a clean and disinfected glass beaker, heat to 176°F/80°C to melt the waxes. Add phase B to phase A and stir well until the color is uniform, then remove from heat. Add phase C to phase A/B and pour while still hot and liquid into the prepared mold. Top off where it settles. Cool in the refrigerator, then remove lipstick from the mold as shown in the picture series.

Phase A
Polyisobutene-800 41.8% (20.9ml / 4 1/4tsp)

Isoeicosane 18% (9ml / 2tsp)

Microcrystalline Wax 8% (4g / 1 3/4tsp)

Carnauba Wax 7% (3.5g / 1/2Tbsp)

Mica Spheres 5% (2.5g / 1/2Tbsp)

Stearyl Palmitate 2% (1g / 1/2tsp)

Vitamin C L-Ascorbyl Palmitate 1% (0.5g / 1/4tsp)

Phase B
D&C Red No. 7 Dispersion 3% (1.5g / 1/4tsp)

D&C Red No. 6 Dispersion 3% (1.5g / 1/4tsp)

Mica Blackstar Red 2% (1g / 1/2tsp)

Mica Bordeaux 6% (3g / 1 1/2tsp)

Titanium Dioxide Dispersion 2% (1g / 1/4tsp)

Phase C
Vitamin E Tocopherol 0.2% (0.1ml / 2 drops)

Phenoxyethanol-SA 1% (0.5ml / 12 drops)

Flavor (optional)

Rosewood Shine Lipstick
Color: Rosewood, 50 g / 1.8 oz, 8-10 Lipsticks

Shiny color lipstick formulated with jojoba gel that provides body and water resistance. The pigments D&C red No. 6 and 7 are finely dispersed in castor oil and ready to blend with the other pigments. Wear lipstick alone or pair with a lip gloss. Contains a natural sun protection factor of 4-6.

Method: Add phase A into a clean and disinfected glass beaker, heat to 168°F/76°C to melt the waxes. Add phase B to phase A and stir well until the color is uniform. Remove from heat. Add phase C to phase A/B and pour the mixture into the prepared mold while the mixture is still hot and liquid. Top off where it settles. Cool in the refrigerator, then remove lipstick form the mold as shown in the picture series.

Phase A
Jojoba Gel 25% (12.5g / 2 3/4tsp)

Polyisobutene-800 41.8% (20.9ml / 4tsp)

Titanium Dioxide Dispersion 2% (1g / 1/4tsp)

Ozokerite Wax 7% (3.5g / 1 1/2tsp)

Candelilla Wax 9% (4.5g / 1 3/4tsp)

Lanolin Alcohol 2% (1g / 1/4tsp)

Phase B
Iron Oxid Brown Dispersion 2% (1ml / 1/4tsp)

D&C Red No. 7 Dispersion 2% (1ml / 1/4tsp)

D&C Red No. 6 Dispersion 2.5% (1.25ml / 1/4tsp)

Mica Red 5% (2.5g / 1 1/4tsp)

Phase C
Vitamin E Aceate 0.5% (0.25ml / 6 drops)

Vitamin E Tocopherol 0.2% (0.1ml / 2 drops)

Phenoxyethanol-SA 1% (0.5ml / 12 drops)

Flavor (optional)

Sheer Petal Lipstick
Color: Sheer Petal, 50 g / 1.8 oz, 8-10 Lipsticks

This lipstick is formulated with four different waxes for a nice consistency, good texture and pay-off. Tripeptide-5 stimulates collagen synthesis and adds volume to improve the contour of the lips. It can be added to any other formula as well but then omit 2.5% of emollient. Lanolin oil and lanolin alcohol moisturize very well.

Method: Add phase A into a clean and disinfected glass beaker, heat to 176°F/80°C to melt the waxes. Add phase B to phase A and stir well until the color is uniform. Remove from heat. Add phase C to phase A/B and pour while still hot and liquid into the prepared mold. Top off where it settles. Cool in the refrigerator, then remove lipstick from mold as shown in the picture series.

Phase A
Castor Oil 25.3% (12.7ml / 2 1/2tsp)

Triglyceride 16% (8ml / 1/2Tbsp)

Isoeicosane 17% (8.5ml / 1/2Tbsp)

Lanolin Oil 5% (2.5ml / 1/2tsp)

Lanolin Alcohol 5% (2.5g / 3/4tsp)

Microcrystalline Wax 2% (1g / 1/2tsp)

Ozokerite Wax 5% (2.5g / 1tsp)

Candelilla Wax 7% 3.5g/1 1/4tsp

Carnauba Wax 3% (1.5g / 1/2tsp)

Vitamin C L-Ascorbyl Palmitate 0.5% (0.25g / 1/8tsp)

Phase B
D&C Red No. 7 Dispersion 2% (1ml / 1/4tsp)

Mica Carmine Red 5% (2.5g / 1 1/4tsp)

Mica Pearlwhite 6% (3g / 1 1/2tsp)

Phase C
Tripeptide-5 2.5% (1.25ml / 30 drops)

Vitamin E Tocopherol 0.2% (0.1ml / 2 drops)

Phenoxyethanol-SA 1% (0.5ml / 12 drops)

Flavor (optional)

Cocoa Butter Lipstick
Color: Cocoa Berry, 50 g / 1.8 oz, 8-10 Lipsticks

Nice semi-matte lipstick with rich cocoa butter gives lips instant protection and nice coverage. Wear alone or pair with lip shimmer or lip gloss.

Method: Add phase A into clean and disinfected glass beaker, heat to 176°F/80°C to melt the waxes. Add phase B to phase A and stir well until the color is uniform, remove from the heat. Add phase C to phase A/B and pour while still hot and liquid into the prepared mold. Top off where it settles. Cool in the refrigerator, then remove lipstick from mold as shown in the picture series.

Phase A
Castor Oil 22.8% (11.4g / 2 1/4tsp)

Triglyceride 15% (7.5ml / 1/2Tbsp)

Isoeicosane 16% (8ml / 1/2Tbsp)

Polyisobutene-800 5% (2.5ml / 1/2tsp)

Lanolin Alcohol 5% (2.5g / 3/4tsp)

Cocoa Butter 5% (2.5g / 1tsp)

Ozokerite Wax 5% (2.5g / 1tsp)

Carnauba Wax 3% (1.5g / 1/2tsp)

Candelilla Wax 7% (3.5g / 1 1/4tsp)

Vitamin C L-Ascorbyl Palmitate 0.5% (0.25g / 1/8tsp)

Phase B
D&C Red No. 6 Dispersion 2% (1ml / 1/4tsp)

Iron Oxide Brown Dispersion 0.5% (0.25ml / 6 drops)

Mica Pearlwhite 5% (2.5g / 1 1/4tsp)

Mica Bronze 5% (2.5g / 1 1/4tsp)

Mica Carmine Red 2% (1g / 1/2tsp)

Phase C
Vitamin E Tocopherol 0.2% (0.1g / 2 drops)

Phenoxyethanol-SA 1% (0.5ml / 12 drops)

Flavor (optional)

Glossy Lipstick
Color: Pink Berry, 50 g / 1.8 oz, 8-10 Lipsticks

Creamy and glossy color lipstick with sheabutter and jojoba gel that adds moisture, shine and viscosity. Diamond cluster mica adds a noticeable sparkle. Formulated with sun protection and antioxidants to protect the lips. Sun protection factor is 10-15.

Method: Add phase A into clean and disinfected glass beaker, heat to 168°F/76°C to melt the waxes. Add phase B to phase A and stir well until the color is uniform. Remove from the heat. Add phase C to phase A/B and pour while still hot and liquid into the prepared mold. Top off where it settles. Cool in the refrigerator, then remove lipstick from mold as shown in the picture series.

Phase A
Polyisobutene-800 38.5% (19.3g / 4tsp)

Jojoba Gel 20% (10g / 2tsp)

OM-Cinnamate 5% (2.5g / 1/2tsp)

Sheabutter 4% (2g / 1/2tsp)

Candelilla Wax 9% (4.5g / 1/2Tbsp)

Ozokerite Wax 7.5% (3.8g / 1 1/2tsp)

Phase B
D&C Red No. 7 Dispersion 3% (1.5ml / 1/4tsp)

Titanium Dioxide Dispersion 2% (1ml / 1/4tsp)

Mica Bordeaux 3% (1.5g / 3/4tsp)

Mica Pearlwhite 4% (2g / 1tsp)

Mica Diamond Cluster 2% (1g / 1/2tsp)

Phase C
Vitamin E Acetate 0.5% (0.25ml / 6 drops)

Vitamin A Palmitate 0.5% (0.25ml / 6 drops)

Phenoxyethanol-SA 1% (0.5ml / 12 drops)

Flavor (optional)

Vegan Lipstick
Color: Garnet, 50 g / 1.8 oz, 8-10 Lipsticks

Lipstick with three different plant oils, natural waxes and avocado butter. Formulated to give a creamy, comforting and protecting lipstick with rich, full color in garnet.

Method: Add phase A into clean and disinfected glass beaker, heat to 176°F/80°C to melt the waxes. Add phase B to phase A and stir well until the color is uniform. Remove from heat. Add phase C to phase A/B and pour while still hot and liquid into the prepared mold. Top off where it settles. Cool in the refrigerator, then remove lipstick from mold as shown in the picture series.

Phase A
Castor Oil 31.8% (15.9ml / 1Tbsp)

Meadowfoam Seed Oil 17% (8.5ml / 1/2Tbsp)

Jojoba Oil 8% (4ml / 3/4tsp)

Avocado Butter 5% (2.5g / 1/2tsp)

Stearyl Palmitate 3% (1.5g / 1/2tsp)

Candelilla Wax 9.5% (4.75g / 1 3/4tsp)

Carnauba Wax 6% (3g / 1 1/2tsp)

Vitamin C L-Ascorbyl Palmitate 0.5% (0.25g / 1/8tsp)

Phase B
Mica Pearlwhite 7% (3.5g / 1 3/4tsp)

Mica Bordeaux 5% (2.5g / 1 1/4tsp)

D&C Red No. 7 Dispersion 4% (2ml / 1/2tsp)

D&C Red No. 6 Dispersion 2% (1ml / 1/4tsp)

Phase C
Vitamin E Tocopherol 0.2% (0.1ml / 2 drops)

Phenoxyethanol-SA 1% (0.5ml / 12 drops)

Flavor (optional)

Sheer Cassis Lipstick
Color: Cassis, 50 g / 1.8 oz, 8-10 Lipsticks

Formula that gives lips instant polish with rich, full color. Creamy avocado butter, vitamin E and provitamin B5 moisturize and protect the lips. Edelweiss extract is a very effective antioxidant that prevents sun damage to the lips caused by free radical attacks.

Method: Add phase B to a mortar and blend well with the pestle until the iron oxide black is fully dispersed and the color is uniform. Transfer it into a heat resistant glass beaker, (take loss in account and add a bit more of the dispersion and iron oxide black, when mixing in the mortar). Add phase A into the beaker as well and heat to 176°F/80°C to melt the waxes. Add phase C as well and stir. Remove from the heat and pour while still hot and liquid into the prepared mold. Top off where it settles. Cool in the refrigerator, then remove lipstick from mold as shown in the picture series.

Phase A
Castor Oil 22% (11ml / 2 1/4tsp)
Isoeicosane 15% (7.5ml / 1/2Tbsp)
Polyisobutene-800 5% (2.5ml / 1/2tsp)
Lanolin Alcohol 5% (2.5g / 3/4tsp)
Avocado Butter 5% (2.5g / 3/4tsp)
Ozokerite Wax 5% (2.5g / 1tsp)
Carnauba Wax 3% (1.5g / 3/4tsp)
Candelilla Wax 8% (4g / 1/2Tbsp)
Provitamin B5 1% (0.5ml / 1/4tsp)
Vitamin E Acetate 0.5% (0.25ml / 6 drops)

Phase B
Triglyceride 13% (6.5ml / 1 1/2tsp)
D&C Red No. 7 Dispersion 2% (1ml / 1/4tsp)
Iron Oxide Black 0.3% (0.15g / 1/16tsp)

Phase C
Mica Red 8% (4g / 2tsp)
Mica Blackstar Red 3% (1.5g / 3/4tsp)
Edelweiss Extract 3% (1.5ml / 1/4tsp)
Vitamin E Tocopherol 0.2% (0.1g / 2 drops)
Phenoxyethanol-SA 1% (0.5ml / 12 drops)
Flavor (optional)

Sheer Lip Shimmer Stick

Color: Burnt Sugar, 50 g / 1.8 oz, 8-10 Sticks

Creamy formula with just a tint of color. Soothing and moisturizing ingredients such as vitamin E, provitamin B and allantoin provide excellent lip protection while Edelweiss extract acts as strong antioxidant protecting the lips from environmental stress.

Method: Add phase A into a clean and disinfected glass beaker, heat to 168°F/76°C to melt the waxes. Add phase B to phase A and stir for a uniform color. Remove from the heat and add phase C. Stir and pour while still hot and liquid into the prepared mold. Top off where it settles. Cool in the refrigerator, then remove lipstick from mold as shown in the picture series. Alternatively, you can also pour the hot lipstick mass directly into a lip balm container without using a mold.

Phase A
Jojoba Oil 25.8% (12.9ml / 1Tbsp)

Jojoba Gel 34% (17ml / 1Tbsp + 1/2tsp)

Castor Oil 12% (6ml / 1 1/4tsp)

Candelilla Wax 8% (4g / 1/2Tbsp)

Ozokerite Wax 6% (3g / 1 1/4tsp)

Microcrystalline Wax 3% (1.5g / 1/2tsp)

Phase B
Vitamin E Acetate 1% (0.5ml / 12 drops)

Allantoin 0.2% (0.1g / 1/16tsp)

Mica Pearlwhite 2% (1g / 1/2tsp)

Mica Bronze 2% (1g / 1/2tsp)

Mica Bordeaux 1% (0.5g / 1/4tsp)

Phase C
Edelweiss Extract 3% (1.5ml / 1/4tsp)

Provitamin B5 1% (0.5ml / 12 drops)

Phenoxyethanol-SA 1% (0.5ml / 12 drops)

Cocoa Pot Lip Gloss
Color: Brandy, 50 g / 1.8 oz

Solid shiny lip gloss with cocoa butter and jojoba gel that gives shine and thickness. Soothing botanicals including rosehip oil, cocoa butter and jojoba keep the lips soft and supple.

Method: Add phase A into clean and disinfected glass beaker and heat to 176°F/80°C to melt the waxes, stir to mix the ingredients. When melted, add phase B and stir. Remove from the heat, add phase C and stir again, pour while still hot and liquid into lip balm pots or lip balm tubes. Let cool.

Phase A
Polyisobutene-800 40% (20ml / 4tsp)

Jojoba Gel 22.8% (11.4g / 2 1/2tsp)

Rose Hip Oil 10% (5ml / 1tsp)

Microcrystalline Wax 7% (3.5g / 1 1/2tsp)

Cacao Butter 7% (3.5g / 1/2Tbsp)

Carnauba Wax 5% (2.5g / 1tsp)

Phase B
Iron Oxide Brown Dispersion 1% (0.5ml / 1/8tsp)

D&C Red No. 7 Dispersion 1% (0.5ml / 1/8tsp)

Mica Red 3% (1.5g / 3/4tsp)

Mica Carmine Red 1% (0.5g / 1/4tsp)

Titanium Dioxide Dispersion 1% (0.5g / 1/8tsp)

Phase C
Vitamin E Tocopherol 0.2% (0.1g / 2 drops)

Phenoxyethanol-SA 1% (0.5ml / 12 drops)

Flavor (optional)

Sun Sparkle Lip Glaze
Color: Rose Gold, 50 ml / 1.7 floz, 4-6 Vials

This lip glaze has nice sparkle and can be worn alone or layered over lip color. Jojoba gel provides a nice viscosity and a high shine. The glaze has a tint of rose-gold and contains two sunscreens which give a sun protection factor of 12-15.

Method: Add the ingredients of phase A into a clean and disinfected glass beaker and stir well to disperse the sunscreens. Add phase B one by one and stir well until the color is uniform. The color can be intensified further by adding more of the mica pigments. Transfer the lip gloss to the lip gloss vial using a pipette or a syringe. The lip glaze is very viscous; it helps to heat it to 130°F/55°C to make it a little more liquid for easier packaging.

Phase A
Jojoba Gel 69.7% (34.9g / 2 1/2Tbsp)

Polyisobutene-250 20% (10ml / 2tsp)

OM-Cinnamate 5% (2.5ml / 1/2tsp)

Titanium Dioxide Dispersion 2% (1ml / 1/4tsp)

Phase B
Mica Carmine Red 1% (0.5g / 1/4tsp)

Mica Gold 3% (1.5g / 3/4tsp)

Vitamin E Acetate 0.5% (0.25g / 6 drops)

Vitamin E Tocopherol 0.2% (0.1ml / 2 drops)

Phenoxyethanol-SA 1% (0.5ml / 12 drops)

Flavor (optional)

Shimmer Lip Gloss "Barely There"

Color: Nude Shimmer, 50 ml / 1.7 floz, 4-6 Vials

This recipe gives a lip gloss that is barely visible but highlights the natural tone of your lips with a slight shimmer. While the micas provide shimmer, polyisobutene and castor oil add also shine. Microcrystalline wax gives thickness for a pleasant application. The formula also contains vitamin C and vitamin E for antioxidant protection.

Method: Add phase A into a clean and disinfected glass beaker and heat to 168°F/ 76°C to melt the wax, stir until uniform, then remove from the heat. Add phase B to phase A and stir. Color can be intensified further by adding more of the mica pigments. Fill the lip gloss while still hot into vials using a pipette or a syringe. Let cool.

Phase A
Polyisobutene-800 30% (15ml / 1Tbsp)

Castor Oil 25.3% (12.7ml / 2 1/2tsp)

Jojoba Oil 35% (17.5ml / 1Tbsp + 1/2tsp)

Microcrystalline Wax 2.5% (1.25g / 1/2tsp)

Vitamin C L-Ascorbyl Palmitate 0.5% (0.25g / 1/8tsp)

Mica Pearlwhite 3% (1.5g / 3/4tsp)

Mica Oriental Beige 1% (0.5g / 1/4tsp)

Mica Bordeaux 1.5% (0.75g / 1/2tsp)

Phase B
Vitamin E Tocopherol 0.2% (0.1ml / 2 drops)

Phenoxyethanol-SA 1% (0.5ml / 12 drops)

Flavor (optional)

Jojoba Lip Glaze
Color: Blackstar Red, 50 ml / 1.7 floz, 4-6 Vials

This lip glaze is based on two different jojoba products, jojoba gel and jojoba oil. Jojoba gel is a very viscous, clear oil and is used in many recipes because it provides a noticeable shine and is also an excellent emollient. In addition, jojoba gel has good water proving properties, is long lasting on the lips and not tacky at all.

Method: Add phase A into a disinfected glass beaker and stir well. Add phase B to phase A and mix the ingredients until uniform. Color can be adjusted by adding more of the mica pigments or pigment dispersions. Transfer the lip gloss to the lip gloss vial using a pipette or a syringe. As the glaze is very viscous, it is best to heat it to 130°F/55°C to make it a little more liquid for easier packaging.

Phase A
Jojoba Gel 77% (38.5g / 2Tbsp + 2tsp)
Jojoba Oil 14% (7ml / 1 1/2tsp)
Vitamin E Acetate 0.5% (0.25g / 6 drops)
Vitamin E Tocopherol 0.5% (0.25g / 6 drops)

Phase B
D&C Red No. 7 Dispersion 0.5% (0.25ml / 1/16tsp)
Iron Oxide Brown Dispersion 0.5% (0.25ml / 1/16tsp)
Mica Pearlwhite 4% (2g / 1tsp)
Mica Blackstar Red 2% (1g / 1/2tsp)
Phenoxyethanol-SA 1% (0.5ml / 12 drops)
Flavor (optional)

Crystal Lip Gloss

Color: Colorless, 50 ml / 1.7 floz, 4-6 Vials

This is a colorless high-shine lip gloss for a translucent look or over lipstick to seal the color. The gloss softens, protects and heals dry lips with the help of vitamin E and provitamin B5.

Method: Add the ingredients one by one into a clean and disinfected glass beaker and stir well to mix all the ingredients. Transfer the lip gloss to the lip gloss vial using a pipette or a syringe. As the lip gloss is very viscous, it is best to heat it to 130°F/55°C to make it a little more liquid for easier packaging.

Phase A

Jojoba Gel 77% (38.5g / 2Tbsp + 2tsp)

Jojoba Oil 20% (10ml / 2tsp)

Provitamin B5 1% (0.5ml / 12 drops)

Vitamin E Acetate 1% (0.5ml / 12 drops)

Phenoxyethanol-SA 1% (0.5ml / 12 drops)

Flavor (optional)

Tint of Pink Lip Gloss
Color: Pink Sugar, 50 ml / 1.7 floz, 4-6 Vials

Clusters of mica give sparkle to this shiny lip gloss while bordeaux mica provides a tint of pink. Tripeptide-5 is an active ingredient that stimulates collagen synthesis and adds volume to improve the contour of the lips.

Method: Add the ingredients of Phase A into a clean and disinfected glass beaker and stir well to mix the ingredients. Add phase B to phase A and mix until uniform. Color can be adjusted by adding more of the mica pigments. Transfer the lip gloss to the lip gloss vial using a pipette. As the gloss is very viscous, it is best to heat it to 130°F/55°C to make it a little more liquid for easier packaging.

Phase A
Jojoba Gel 70% (35.1g / 2 1/2Tbsp)
Jojoba Oil 19% (9.5ml / 2tsp)
Titanium Dioxide Dispersion 1% (0.5g / 1/8tsp)
Vitamin E Acetate 1% (0.5ml / 12 drops)

Phase B
Mica Diamond Cluster 3% (1.5g / 3/4tsp)
Mica Pearlwhite 1% (0.5g / 1/4tsp)
Mica Bordeaux 2% (1g / 1/2tsp)
Tripeptide-5 3% (1.5ml / 1/4tsp)
Phenoxyethanol-SA 1% (0.5ml / 12 drops)
Flavor (optional)

Extra Moisturizing Lip Balm

100 g / 3.6 oz, 10-15 Lip Balms

Easy lip balm that retains moisture, reduces transepidermal water loss, comforts and protects the lips for many hours.

Method: Add the ingredients of phase A to a clean and disinfected glass beaker and heat to 170°F/76°C until the waxes are melted, stir and remove from the heat. Add phase B and stir, pour directly while still hot and liquid into lip balm tubes, pots or a mold. Let cool. If you want to make only 5-7 lip balms (50g), simply divide the amounts of the ingredients by two.

Phase A

Vaseline 44% (44g / 3 3/4Tbsp)

Jojoba Oil 22% (22g / 1 1/2Tbsp)

Almond Oil 13% (13g / 1Tbsp)

Candelilla Wax 8% (8g / 1Tbsp)

Ozokerite Wax 8% (8g / 1Tbsp)

Avocado Butter 3% (3g / 3/4tsp)

Phase B

Provitamin B5 0.5% (0.5g / 12 drops)

Vitamin E Acetate 0.5% (0.5g / 12 drops)

Phenoxyethanol-SA 1% (1ml / 24 drops)

Flavor (optional)

Buttery Lip Balm with Sun Protection
100 g / 3.6 oz, 10-15 Lip Balms

Lip care stick formulated with cocoa butter, avocado butter, natural jojoba and three different vitamins. It leaves the lips soft and smooth and provides velvety. Contains a sun protection factor of 15-18.

Method: Add the ingredients of phase A to a clean and disinfected glass beaker and heat to 168°F/76°C until the waxes are melted. Stir and remove from heat. Add phase B and stir, pour directly while still hot and liquid into lip balm tubes or pots. Let cool. If you want to make only 5-7 lip balms (50g), simply divide the amounts of the ingredients by two.

Phase A
Jojoba Oil 46.3% (46.3g / 3Tbsp + 1/4tsp)

Meadowfoam Seed Oil 20% (20g / 4tsp)

Cocoa Butter 6% (6g / 3/4Tbsp)

Avocado Butter 5% (5g / 1 1/4tsp)

Bees Wax 7% (7g / 1Tbsp + 1/2tsp)

Ozokerite Wax 5% (5g / 2tsp)

Titanium Dioxide Dispersion 3% (3g / 3/4tsp)

OM-Cinnamate 5% (5g / 1tsp)

Phase B
Provitamin B5 1% (1g / 24 drops)

Vitamin E Acetate 0.5% (0.5g / 12 drops)

Vitamin E Tocopherol 0.2% (0.2g / 5 drops)

Phenoxyethanol-SA 1% (1ml / 24 drops)

Flavor (optional)

Lip Moisture Stick
100 g / 3.6 oz, 10-15 Lip Balms

Lip care stick with high protection against UVA and UVB rays. Can be worn over lipstick or just bare. Triglyceride is a good solvent for UV-filters. Edelweiss extract is a very effective antioxidant that soothes UV-stressed skin and neutralizes free radicals to prevent sun damage to the skin cells. Sun protection factor is 24-28.

Method: Add the ingredients of phase A to a clean and disinfected glass beaker and heat to 176°F/80°C until the waxes are melted, stir and remove from the heat. Add phase B and stir, pour directly while still hot and liquid into lip balm tubes or pots. Let cool. If you want to make only 5-7 lip balms (50g), simply divide the amounts of the ingredients by two.

Phase A
Triglyceride 34% (34ml / 2Tbsp + 1tsp)

Jojoba Oil 30.5% (30ml / 2Tbsp)

Sheabutter 5% (5g / 1 1/4tsp)

OM-Cinnamate 7.5% (7.5g / 1/2Tbsp)

Oxybenzone 2% (2g / 1/2tsp)

Titanium Dioxide Dispersion 3% (3g / 3/4tsp)

Carnauba Wax 6.5% (6.5g / 3/4Tbsp)

Microcrystalline Wax 7% (7g / 1Tbsp)

Phase B
Edelweiss Extract 3% (3ml / 1/2tsp)

Vitamin E Acetate 0.5% (0.5g / 12 drops)

Phenoxyethanol-SA 1% (1ml / 24 drops)

Flavor (optional)

Lip Balm with Golden Shine

100 g / 3.6 oz, 10-15 Lip Balms

Solid balm for long-lasting soft lips. Adds gloss to lips with a hint of gold. Meadowfoam seed oil is a very stable oil that makes it a very valuable ingredient in lip care products. As the recipe on page 120, liquid titanium dioxide dispersion is added for UV protection. Sun protection factor is 4-6.

Method: Add the ingredients of phase A to a clean and disinfected glass beaker and heat to 170°F/76°C until the waxes are melted, stir and remove from the heat. Add phase B and stir, pour directly while still hot and liquid into lip balm tubes or pots. Let cool. If you want to make only 5-7 lip balms (50g), simply divide the amounts of the ingredients by two.

Phase A

Meadowfoam Seed Oil 42% (42ml / 2Tbsp + 2tsp)

Castor Oil 25% (30ml / 2Tbsp)

Isoeicosane 9% (9g / 2 1/4tsp)

Microcrystalline Wax 8% (8g / 1Tbsp + 1/2tsp)

Candelilla Wax 6% (6g / 2 1/4tsp)

Cetyl Alcohol 3 % (3g / 1tsp)

Vitamin E Acetate 1% (1g / 24 drops)

Titanium Dioxide Dispersion 2% (2ml / 1/2tsp)

Phase B

Mica Gold 3% (3g / 1 1/2tsp)

Phenoxyethanol-SA 1% (1ml / 24 drops)

Flavor (optional)

Cosmetic Pencils

Introduction

Cosmetic pencils are used as lip, brow and eyeliners.

Lip Liners: Ideally, lip liners should have high pigment coverage to accent the line of the lip, and should be firm enough not to run into the lines around the lip. Lip liners should also be suitable for drawing a thin, clearly defined line around the periphery of the lips.

Eye Brow Liners: Brow liners are used to create the illusion of fuller brows or to cover areas that have no hair. Good brow liners give a smooth, even coverage that gently shapes and defines brows, and won't sweat off. Brow liners are usually harder than lip or eyeliners.

Eyeliners: Ideally, eyeliners should glide on without tugging or pulling on the eyelid on application. This can be achieved by making an eyeliner not too hard. It should, however, also not be too soft, since the depth of color should be controllable during application. Traditionally, colors for eyeliners included primarily black, black-blues, black-greens and violet. Todays' eyeliners, however, come in a wide color range with all kinds of shades.

Formulation

Cosmetic pencils consist mainly of waxes, oils, and pigments. Good pigment coverage is essential, whereas emolliency is not necessary. For this reason, the wax/pigment level is relatively high, whereas the oil level is rather low. A high pigment load necessitates a somewhat longer, and more intense, wetting and milling procedure with the mortar and pestle to make sure that pigment clumps are broken and the particles are dispersed finely.

Formulas for brow liners contain generally less pigments as they are designed to tint rather than color. Their color payoff is therefore reduced.

Waxes used for cosmetic pencils include candelilla wax, carnauba wax, beeswax, ozokerit, microcrystalline wax and Japan wax. The amount of waxes in pencils is in the range of 20-40%. Often stearic acid is used along with waxes to provide a firmer structure.

Oils are needed to wet and disperse the pigments. Both plant oils and synthetic oils (e.g. triglyceride) can be used. The amount of oils often totals as much as 25% of the formula because pigments absorb oils and are used at rather high concentrations.

Sometimes texturizers like talc or silica powders are used to add consistency to the formula. Furthermore, skin-benefiting ingredients like vitamin E, vitamin C and provitamin B5 are increasingly incorporated.

The most frequently used pigments for lip liners are organic pigments (e.g. D&C red 6 & 7) and less frequently used are micas in various shades. For eyeliners dark colored inorganic pigments like iron oxides (e.g. black, brown) and ultramarines (e.g. ultramarine blue) are typically used. Be aware that some organic pigments are not allowed to use in the eye area (e.g. D&C red 6, 7, 21, 22, 27 or D&C green 6 & 8). For eye brow liners also iron oxides are used.

Filling Pencils

Pencils are manufactured by injecting the mass directly into the hollow barrel. This is done easily with a medical syringe. The syringe is stuck into one end of the pencil and the hot mass is then slowly injected without interruption. Hold the pencil horizontally. Rotate the pencil a few times while filling to make sure that the pencil is filled evenly. The pencil is filled completely when the liquid starts to dripping out of the other end. Remove the syringe and keep the pencil horizontally for a couple more minutes to avoid the filling to drip out.

The mass starts to harden quickly but will require at least half an hour in the refrigerator until it is hard enough for sharpening. The filling in the pencil may continue to harden completely in the next few days.

It is easiest to fill pencils with the hot mass using a medical syringe.

The pencil is filled completely when the filling starts dripping out of the pencil. Fill the pencil without interrupting.

Lip Liner Pencil (1)
Color: Raspberry, 50 g / 1.8 oz, 10-15 Slim Pencils

Lip liner pencil for a perfect definition of your lips. It goes on smoothly and evenly. Formulated with jojoba oil, a red color dispersion and red mica pigments.

Method: Combine the ingredients of phase A in a heat resistant glass beaker and stir, heat to 185°F/85°C to melt the waxes. Add phase B to phase A and stir until the color is uniform; remove from heat. While still hot and liquid, fill into empty pencil bodies as shown in the pictures. The formulation can be adjusted by adding more waxes to make the pencil harder or more jojoba oil to make it softer.

Phase A
Carnauba Wax 8% (4g / 2tsp)

Microcrystalline Wax 4% (2g / 3/4tsp)

Beeswax 12% (6g / 1Tbsp)

Cetyl Alcohol 7% (3.5g / 1 1/2tsp)

Vitamin C L-Ascorbyl Palmitate 0.5% (0.25g / 1/8tsp)

Phase B
Red D&C No. 6 Dispersion 9% (4.5ml / 3/4tsp)

Mica Red 16% (8g / 4tsp)

Jojoba Gel 23% (11.5g / 2 1/4tsp)

Jojoba Oil 20% (10ml / 2tsp)

Vitamin E Acetate 0.5% (0.25g / 6 drops)

Lip Liner Pencil (II)

Color: Rum, 50 g / 1.8 oz, 10-15 Slim Pencils

Nice lip liner pencil in rum color to define your lips. The color is made by using two different iron oxide dispersions and mica red. Instead of waxes, stearic acid and cetyl alcohol are used.

Method: Combine the ingredients of phase A in a heat resistant glass beaker and stir, heat to 158°F/70°C to melt the solids. Add phase B to phase A and stir until the color is uniform, remove from the heat. While still hot and liquid fill into empty pencil bodies as shown in the pictures. The formulation can be adjusted by adding more stearic acid to make the pencil harder or more jojoba gel to make it softer.

Phase A
Stearic Acid 40% (20g / 2 1/2Tbsp)
Cetyl Alcohol 10% (5g / 2tsp)
Jojoba Gel 8% (4g / 3/4tsp)

Phase B
Iron Oxide Brown Dispersion 9% (4.5ml / 3/4tsp)
D&C Red No. 7 Dispersion 3% (1.5ml / 1/4tsp)
Mica Red 10% (5g / 2 1/2tsp)
Mica Powder 20% (10g / 3Tbsp + 1tsp)
Vitamin E Tocopherol 0.2% (0.1g / 2 drops)

Lip Liner Pencil (III)
Color: Mauve, 50 g / 1.8 oz, 10-15 Slim Pencils

This creamy lip liner goes on smoothly and evenly to give lips subtle definition. Mauve is a color that suits almost anyone.

Method: Combine the ingredients of phase A in a heat resistant glass beaker and stir, heat to 185°F/85°C to melt the waxes. Add phase B to phase A and stir until the color is uniform; remove from heat. While still hot and liquid, fill into empty pencil bodies as shown in the pictures. The formulation can be adjusted by adding more waxes to make the pencil harder or more triglyceride to make it softer.

Phase A
Meadowfoam Seed Oil 32.8% (16.6g / 1Tbsp + 1/2tsp)

Triglyceride 10% (5g / 1tsp)

Bees Wax 11% (5.5g / 2 1/2tsp)

Carnauba Wax 9% (4.5g / 2tsp)

Cetyl Alcohol 10% (5g / 2tsp)

Phase B
Iron Oxide Brown Dispersion 10% (5ml / 1tsp)

D&C Red No. 7 Dispersion 3% (1.5ml / 1/4tsp)

Mica Carmine Red 8% (4g / 2tsp)

Mica Pearlwhite 6% (3g / 1 1/2tsp)

Vitamin E Tocopherol 0.2% (0.1g / 2 drops)

Eye Shadow Pencil (1)

Color: Violet, 50 g / 1.8 oz, 10-15 Slim Pencils

Accentuate the eyes with a violet look! Use on upper and lower lid for a nice effect. It looks great with brown and natural shades. Formula can be used for thick crayons or slim pencils or can even be poured into a slim lip container. Apply directly on the lid.

Method: Add phase A into a heat resistant glass beaker. Add phase B into a mortar and blend well with the pestle until the color is uniform, add to phase A. Heat the beaker to 185°F/85°C to melt the waxes. Stir until uniform. When completely melted, remove from the heat. While still hot and liquid fill into empty pencil bodies as shown in the pictures. The formulation can be adjusted by adding more waxes to make the pencil harder or more isoeicosane to make it softer.

Phase A
Polyisobutene-250 33.5% (16.8g / 1Tbsp + 1/4tsp)

Beeswax 5% (2.5g / 1 1/4tsp)

Candelilla Wax 4% (2g / 3/4tsp)

Isoeicosane 8.5% (4.3ml / 1tsp)

Triglyceride 9% (4.5ml / 1tsp)

Carnaubawax 4% (2g / 1tsp)

Cetyl Alcohol 5% (2.5g / 1tsp)

BHT 0.2% (0.1g / 1/16tsp)

Phase B
Ultramarine Blue 2.8% (1.4g / 1/2tsp)

Mica Magenta 24% (12g / 2Tbsp)

Mica Carmine Red 4% (2g / 1tsp)

Eye Shadow Pencil (II)
Color: Sand Gold, 50 g / 1.8 oz, 10-15 Slim Pencils

This formula gives a long-wearing, water-resistant pencil for lining the eyes. The soft color illuminates the eye with a shiny sand gold shade.

Method: Combine the ingredients of phase B into a heat resistant glass beaker and stir to mix the pigments. Add phase A to it and heat to 185°F/85°C to melt the waxes. When completely melted, stir and remove from heat. While still hot and liquid, fill into empty pencil bodies as shown in the pictures. The formulation can be adjusted by adding more waxes to make the pencil harder or more triglyceride to make it softer.

Phase A
Beeswax 11% (5.5g / 1Tbsp)
Cetyl Alcohol 5% (2.5g / 1tsp)
Microcrystalline Wax 3% (1.5g / 1/2tsp)
Carnauba Wax 5% (2.5g / 1 1/4tsp)
Polyisobutene-800 27% (13.5ml / 3/4Tbsp)
Triglyceride 9.8% (4.9ml / 1tsp)
BHT 0.2% (0.1g / 1/16tsp)

Phase B
Mica Powder 15% (7.5g / 2 1/2Tbsp)
Mica Oriental Beige 12% (6g / 3tsp)
Mica Gold 12% (6g / 3tsp)

130

Eyeliner Pencil
Color: Black, 50 g / 1.8 oz, 10-15 Slim Pencils

Long-wearing, water-resistant pencil in classic black. A must-have to accentuate the eyes. Contains provitamin B5 which has conditioning and moisturizing properties.

Method: Add phase A into a heat resistant glass beaker and heat to 158°F/70°C to melt the solid ingredients. Add phase B to phase A and stir well until the color is uniform.

Remove from the heat and add phase C; stir. While still hot and liquid, fill into empty pencil bodies as shown in the pictures. The recipe can be adjusted by adding more stearic acid to make the pencil harder or more polyisobutene to make it softer.

Phase A
Stearic Acid 34.8% (17.4g / 2Tbsp + 1/2tsp)

Polyisobutene-800 24% (12.5ml / 2 1/2tsp)

Cetyl Alcohol 10% (5g / 2tsp)

Phase B
Iron Oxide Black 30% (15g / 1 1/2Tbsp)

Phase C
Polyglyceryl Oleate 0.5% (0.25ml / 6 drops)

Vitamin E Tocopherol 0.2% (0.1ml / 2 drops)

Provitamin B5 0.5% (0.25ml / 6 drops)

Eye Brow Pencil

Color: Espresso, 50 g / 1.8 oz, 10-15 Slim Pencils

Pencil that is used mainly for eyebrows as its consistency and texture is somewhat harder than for eyeliner pencils.

Method: Combine the ingredients of phase B in a mortar, and blend well with the pestle until the color is uniform. Add phase A into a heat resistant glass beaker and heat to 158°F/70°C to melt the solid ingredients.

When melted, add phase B and stir well until the pigments are dispersed. Remove from the heat and add phase C; stir. While still hot and liquid, fill into empty pencil bodies as shown in the pictures. The recipe can be adjusted by adding more stearic acid to make the pencil harder or more jojoba gel to make it softer.

Phase A
Stearic Acid 39.3% (19.7g / 2 1/2Tbsp)

Jojoba Gel 20% (10g / 2tsp)

Cetyl Alcohol 10% (5g / 2tsp)

Phase B
Iron Oxide Brown 15% (7.5g / 1 3/4tsp)

Iron Oxide Black 15% (7.5g / 1 3/4tsp)

Phase C
Vitamin E Tocopherol 0.2% (0.1ml / 2 drops)

Provitamin B5 0.5% (0.25ml / 6 drops)

Eye Shadows

Introduction

The most popular forms of eye shadows are pressed or lose powders, pigmented gels and creams, and sticks. Ideally, eye shadows blend and glide on easily, give high color coverage and stay true for long hours.

Formulation

Powder Eye shadow: The formulation of powder eye shadow does not differ greatly from face powders. The basic ingredients for both pressed and loose powders are mainly pigments, emollients, and texturizers.

Pigments primarily include inorganic colors such as iron oxides, ultramarines and micas, which are not restricted for use in the eye area. Micas are especially useful, as they are available in a wide range of different shades and provide shimmer and special light-diffusing effects. Organic colors can also be used, but many of them are not allowed for eye shadows. Examples of such restricted colors are FD&C green 3 & 6, D&C green 6 & 8, D&C red 6, 7, 21, 22, 27, 28, & 30 (see page 30).

Emollients are needed to wet and disperse the pigments and to hold the powder together which is especially important for making pressed powders. Emulsifiers are also helpful to bind powders. Both plant oils and synthetic oils (e.g. triglyceride) can be used.

Texturizers are important ingredients providing consistency, body, and shimmer to powders. They also help to dilute the colors making them less intense. Typical texturizers used for eye shadows are micas, corn starch, talc, bismuth oxychloride, and magnesium stearate. Particularly, magnesium stearate is a valuable ingredient as it allows the eye shadow to adhere to the skin.

Cream & Gel Eye shadow: In contrast to powder eye shadow (which consists solely of pigments, emollients, and texturizers), eye shadows in cream form are mainly emulsions.

As described previously, emulsions typically consist of a water phase and oil phase, which are held together with one or more emulsifiers. Likewise, eye shadows in gel form contain water, emollients, emulsifiers, and additionally, gelling agents. Such gelling agents are typically polymers (e.g. carbomers or acrylate polymers like GelMaker EMU), which also have thickening and emulsifying properties allowing a reduction in the amount of emulsifiers and emollients.

Pigments are added either to the water or oil phase, depending on the type of emulsion. There are also eye shadows in cream form that are made without water. They are called cream-to-powder eye shadows, as they look like compressed powder cakes but are creamy to apply. Besides emollients, texturizers, and pigments, cream-to-powder eye shadows contain also waxes.

Stick Eye shadow: Similar to other stick cosmetics like lipsticks, stick eye shadows contain a significant amount of waxes. This is necessary to give the stick strength, hardness, and consistency. Texturizers, emollients, and pigments make up the other ingredients.

Loose Mineral Eye Shadow (I)
Color: Your Choice, 30 g / 1.0 oz

Silky eye shadow powder that glides on smoothly and blends easily. Formula allows to create a wide range of shades for lids and lining eyes. Mineral content is 100%.

Method: Combine all ingredients of phase A in a mortar and blend them with the pestle. This base serves as a base for making small quantities and different colors. Use as much as you need from the base and mix with your desired mica pigment(s), or follow the recipe and choose a mica pigment color for phase B. When adding phase B to the mortar blend gently. Prolonged blending would damage the glitter of the micas. Fill finished powder into small sifter jars.

Phase A
Magnesium Stearate 4% (1.2g / 1/2tsp)
Mica Powder 50% (15g / 4Tbsp)
Mica Spheres 20% (6g / 1 1/2Tbsp)

Phase B
Mica Pigment(s) of your choice 16% (4.8g / 2 1/4tsp)
Mica Pearlwhite 10% (3g / 1 1/2tsp)

Loose Mineral Eye Shadow (II)

Color: Gold, 30 g / 1.0 oz

A simple, modern way to wear shimmer. This sheer powder is lightly pearlized to softly illuminate the lids. You can use the shade on lids, as shimmery liner, or highlighter shade under browbone. Gold mica is mixed with oriental beige for a warm gold tone. Mineral content is 100%.

Method: Add phase A into a mortar and blend with the pestle until uniform. Add phase B to the mortar and blend gently. Prolonged blending would damage the glitter of the micas. Fill finished powder into small sifter jars.

Phase A
Talc 29% (8.7g / 1Tbsp)
Mica Powder 28% (8.4g / 2 3/4Tbsp)
Magnesium Stearate 5% (1.5g / 3/4tsp)
Bismuth Oxychloride 6% (1.8g / 3/4tsp)

Phase B
Mica Gold 22% (6.6g / 1Tbsp + 1/4tsp)
Mica Oriental Beige 10% (3g / 1 1/2tsp)

Loose Mineral Eye Shadow (III)
Color: Orchid, 30 g / 1.0 oz

This sheer orchid eye shade flatters a wide range of skin tone. It can be used as shadow for the lids, to line the eyes or as a highlighter under the browbone. Magenta violet is blended with ultramarines to create this fresh orchid shade. A volatile emollient adds a silky touch. Mineral content is 98%.

Method: Add phase A into a mortar and blend well with the pestle until the color is uniform. Add phase B and blend until uniform. Add phase C to the mortar and blend until evenly mixed. Then add phase D to the mortar and blend gently, prolonged blending would damage the glitter of the mica. Fill powder into small sifter jars.

Phase A
Magnesium Stearate 4% (1.2g / 1/2tsp)
Ultramarine Pink 10% (3g / 1 1/4tsp)
Ultramarine Blue 8% (2.4g / 1tsp)

Phase B
Mica Spheres 20% (6g / 1 1/2Tbsp)
Mica Powder 51% (15.5g / 5Tbsp)

Phase C
Cyclo-Dimethicone 2% (0.6ml / 14drops)

Phase D
Mica Magenta 5% (1.5g / 3/4tsp)

Loose Mineral Eye Shadow (IV)
Color: Rose-Gold, 30 g / 1.0 oz

Loose blendable shimmer powder shadow that stays flawless and beautiful to accentuate under browbone or all over lid. Mica red and gold give a warm rose-gold color. Mineral content is 95%.

Method: Add phase A into a mortar and blend well with the pestle until uniform. Add phase B to the mortar and blend gently. Prolonged blending would damage the glitter of the micas. Fill powder into small sifter jars.

Phase A
Corn Starch AS 5% (1.5g / 1/2tsp)
Talc 21% (6.3g / 2 1/4tsp)
Mica Powder 38% (11.4g / 3 3/4Tbsp)
Magnesium Stearate 6% (1.8g / 3/4tsp)

Phase B
Mica Red 15% (4.5g / 2 1/4tsp)
Mica Gold 15% (4.5g / 2 1/4tsp)

Loose Sparkle Mineral Eye Shadow

Color: Silver-Snow, 30 g / 1.0 oz

Eye shadow with silver sparkles that are well noticeable. Useful to accentuate the lids or browbone. Contains pearlwhite, patina silver and semi-white mica. Corn starch is added as oil absorber. Mineral content is 93%.

Method: Add phase A into a mortar and blend with the pestle until uniform. Add phase B to the mortar and blend gently. Prolonged blending would damage the glitter of the micas. Fill powder into small sifter jars.

Phase A
Mica Powder 42% (12.6g / 4Tbsp)

Bismuth Oxychloride 10% (3g / 1 1/4tsp)

Corn Starch AS 7% (2.1g / 3/4tsp)

Mangesium Stearate 5% (1.5g / 3/4tsp)

Phase B
Mica Pearlwhite 20% (6g / 3tsp)

Mica Diamond Cluster 11% (3.3g / 1tsp)

Mica Patina Silver 5% (1.5g / 3/4tsp)

Pressed Mineral Eye Shadow (I)

Color: Mint, 30 g / 1.0 oz

Lightly pearlized, pressed eye shadow to softly illuminate lids. Use shade all over lid or as a highlighter shade under browbone. Emollient and emulsifier act as binders and help to make the eye shadow press better into pots or pans. Mica spheres give the eye shadow a velvet feel. Mineral content is 92.5%.

Method: Add phase A into a mortar. Add phase B one by one to the mortar as well and blend with the pestle between each ingredient until the color is uniform and the emollients are well mixed. Add phase C to the mortar and blend gently. Prolonged blending would damage the glitter of the micas. Press into pots or pans.

Phase A
Cyclo-Dimethicone 7% (2.1g / 1/2tsp)

Polyglyceryl Oleate 0.5% (0.15ml / 4 drops)

Phase B
Magnesium Stearate 3% (0.9g / 1/2tsp)

Chromium Oxide Green 3% (0.9g / 1/4tsp)

Talc 45% (13.5g / 1 3/4Tbsp)

Mica Powder 10% (3g / 1Tbsp)

Mica Spheres 17.5% (5.25g / 1Tbsp + 1tsp)

Phase C
Mica Diamond Cluster 5% (1.5g / 3/4tsp)

Mica Majestic Green 6% (1.8g / 1tsp)

Mica Patina Silver 3% (0.9g / 1/2tsp)

Pressed Mineral Eye Shadow (II)

Color: Sandstorm, 30 g / 1.0 oz

Eye shadow in the color of the Orient. Can be used all over eye lid or just for accentuating. Provides long wear. Contains vitamin E as antioxidant. Eye shadow can be pressed into pots or pans. Mineral content is 95%.

Method: Add phase A into a mortar and blend well with the pestle until the color is uniform. Add phase B to the mortar and blend with the pestle until uniform and the emollients are well mixed. Add phase C and blend well. Add phase D to the mortar and blend gently. Prolonged blending would damage the glitter of the micas. Press into pots or pans.

Phase A
Magnesium Stearate 5% (1.5g / 3/4tsp)

Iron Oxide Black 2% (0.6g / 1/4tsp)

Phase B
Triglyceride 4% (1.2ml / 1/4tsp)

Polyisobutene-250 3% (0.9ml / 22 drops)

Polyglyceryl Oleate 0.8% (0.24ml / 5 drops)

Vitamin E Acetate 0.5% (0.15ml / 4 drops)

Phase C
Mica Powder 39.7% (11.9g / 4Tbsp)

Bismuth Oxychloride 5% (1.5g / 1/2tsp)

Phase D
Mica Oriental Beige 30% (9g / 1 1/2Tbsp)

Mica Pearlwhite 10% (3g / 1 1/2tsp)

Pressed Mineral Eye Shadow (III)
Color: Nude, 30 g / 1.0 oz

Lightly pearlized shade in "nude" color. Use as a base color all over lid or to highlight browbones. Looks clean and fresh and provides long wear. Contains vitamin E as antioxidant. Eye shadow can be pressed into pots or pans. Mineral content is 91%.

Method: Add phase A into a mortar and blend well with the pestle until the color is uniform. Add phase B to the mortar and blend with the pestle until uniform and the emollients are well mixed. Add phase C and blend well. Add phase D to the mortar and blend gently. Prolonged blending would damage the glitter of the micas. Press into pots or pans.

Phase A
Magnesium Stearate 5% (1.5g / 3/4tsp)
Bismuth Oxychloride 5% (1.5g / 1/2tsp)
Titanium Dioxide 5% (1.5g / 1/2tsp)

Phase B
Triglyceride 4% (1.2ml / 1/4tsp)
Polyisobutene-250 3% (0.9ml / 22 drops)
Polyglyceryl Oleate 0.8% (0.24ml / 5 drops)
Vitamin E Acetate 0.5% (0.15ml / 4 drops)

Phase C
Talc or Mica Powder 40.7% (12g / 4Tbsp)

Phase D
Mica Pearlwhite 30% (9g / 1 1/2Tbsp)
Mica Oriental Beige 6% (1.8g / 3/4tsp)

142

Pressed Mineral Eye Shadow (IV)

Color: Chocolate, 30 g / 1.0 oz

Silky, matte formula in chocolate brown. Shadow glides on smoothly and blends easily on lids, lining eyes, and defining brows. Provides long wear. Mineral content is 91.7%.

Method: Add phase A into a mortar and blend well with the pestle until the color is uniform. Add phase B to the mortar and blend with the pestle until uniform and the emollients are well mixed. Add phase C and blend well. Add phase D to the mortar and blend only short, prolong blending would damage the glitter of the micas. Press into pots or pans.

Phase A
Iron Oxide Dark Brown 15% (4.5g / 2 1/4tsp)

Bismuth Oxychloride 5% (1.5g / 1/2tsp)

Magnesium Stearate 5% (1.5g / 3/4tsp)

Iron Oxide Black 5% (1.5g / 1/2tsp)

Phase B
Triglyceride 4% (1.2ml / 1/4tsp)

Polyisobutene-250 3% (0.9ml / 22 drops)

Polyglyceryl Oleate 0.8% (0.24ml / 5 drops)

Vitamin E Acetate 0.5% (0.15ml / 4 drops)

Phase C
Mica Powder 41.7% (12.5g / 4Tbsp)

Phase D
Mica Bronze 10% (3g / 1 1/2tsp)

Mica Pearlwhite 10% (3g / 1 1/2tsp)

Pressed Mineral Eye Shadow (V)

Color: Sheer Lilac, 30 g / 1.0 oz

Silky smooth shadow in a light lilac color which is created by blending gold, bordeaux, white, pink and blue pigments. This soft shade will accentuate every eye. Contains kaolin as oil absorber. Mineral content 94.5%.

Method: Add phase A into a mortar and blend well with the pestle until uniform and free of color streaking. Add phase B to the mortar and blend well. Then add phase C, blend well after each ingredient to receive a uniform color. Add phase D to the mortar and blend gently. Prolonged blending would damage the glitter of the micas. Press into pots or pans.

Phase A
Magnesium Stearate 3% (0.9g / 1/2tsp)

Ultramarine Pink 6% (1.8g / 3/4tsp)

Ultramarine Blue 1% (0.3g / 1/8tsp)

Phase B
Polyisobutene-250 5% (1.5ml / 36 drops)

Polyglyceryl Oleate 0.5% (0.15ml / 5 drops)

Phase C
Kaolin 5% (1.5g / 3/4tsp)

Talc 16% (4.8g / 1 3/4tsp)

Bismuth Oxychloride 5% (1.5g / 1/2tsp)

Mica Powder 29.5% (8.9g / 3Tbsp)

Phase D
Mica Pearlwhite 15% (4.5g / 2 1/4tsp)

Mica Gold 10% (3g / 1 1/2tsp)

Mica Bordeaux 4% (1.2g / 1/2tsp)

Pressed Sheer Mineral Eye Shadow
Color: Pale Pink, 30 g / 1.0 oz

Pressed eye shadow with a fresh and natural pale pink shade. The silky formula glides on smoothly and evenly. Bismuth gives shimmer while carmine mica provide pink sparkle. Nice look that offers long-lasting wear. Mineral content is 92%.

Method: Add phase A into a mortar and blend well to a uniform color. Add phase B to the mortar as well and blend to a uniform color. Then add phase C to the mortar and blend gently. Prolonged blending would damage the glitter of the micas. Press into pots or pans.

Phase A
Talc 32% (9.6g / 3Tbsp)
Bismuth Oxychloride 10% (3g / 1 1/4tsp)
Magnesium Stearate 4% (1.2g / 1/2tsp)
Mica Spheres 15% (4.5g / 1Tbsp + 1/2tsp)
Polyisobutene-250 7% (2.1ml / 1/2tsp)
Polyglyceryl Oleate 1% (0.3ml / 8 drops)

Phase B
Mica Carmine Red 12% (3.6g / 1 3/4tsp)
Mica Magenta 8% (2.4g / 1 1/4tsp)
Mica Red 3% (0.9g / 1/2tsp)

Phase C
Mica Carmine Red 5% (1.5g / 3/4tsp)
Mica Magenta 3% (0.9g / 1/2tsp)

Shimmer Cream Eye Shadow
Color: Glacier Pearl, 30 g / 1.0 oz

This easy and unique long-wearing cream eye shadow highlights every eye. Diamond cluster mica brings high glitter to this formula. It is best applied to the moving eye lid as a touch of sparkle. Dries quickly and does not rub off easily.

Method: Add phase A into a disinfected glass beaker, add phase B, and stir. Add phase C to phase A/B and stir until smooth. Heat to 150°F/65°C. Add phase D into another beaker glass and heat to the same temperature. Add phase D to phase A/B/C and stir well, remove from the heat and let cool while gently stirring. Add phase E and stir well. Fill into small eye shadow jars.

Phase A
Distilled Water 58.8% (17.6ml / 1Tbsp + 1/2tsp)

Phase B
Mica Pearlwhite 20% (6g / 3tsp)
Mica Diamond Cluster 10% (3g / 1tsp)

Phase C
Propylene Glycol 4% (1.2ml / 1/4tsp)

Phase D
Stearic Acid 3.5% (1g / 1/2tsp)
GelMaker EMU 2% (0.6ml / 14 drops)
Cetyl Alcohol 0.5% (0.15g / 1/16tsp)

Phase E
Phenoxyethanol-SA 1.2% (0.4ml / 10 drops)

Shimmer Gel Eye Shadow
Color: Camel, 30 g / 1.0 oz

Gel eye shadow that stays on and is long wearing. This gel formula has a softer consistency than the shimmer cream. White micas and oriental beige blend to a warm camel shade. Use as a base shimmer color or accentuate just the moving eye lid.

Method: Add phase A into a glass beaker and stir. Add phase B to phase A and stir to disperse the Micas. Add phase C to another beaker and blend until uniform. Add phase C to phase A/B and stir well to form an uniform gel. Fill into small eye shadow jars.

Phase A
Distilled Water 62.8% (18.8ml / 1Tbsp + 1/2tsp)

Glycerin 2% (0.6ml / 14 drops)

Phenoxyethanol-SA 1.2% (0.4ml / 10 drops)

Phase B
Mica Pearlwhite 10% (3g / 2 1/2tsp)

Mica Diamond Cluster 5% (1.5g / 1/2tsp)

Mica Oriental Beige 10% (3g / 2 1/2tsp)

Phase C
Iron Oxide Brown Dispersion 1% (0.3ml / 8 drops)

GelMaker EMU 3% (0.9ml / 22 drops)

Triglyceride 5% (1.5ml / 1/4tsp)

Cream Eye Shadow

Color: Ocean (I) or Tawny (II), 30 g / 1.0 oz

Cream eye shadow made with waxes and emollients. After application it dries quickly to a powder. It is soft blending and the color goes on nicely. Choose from two different colors: 'ocean' or 'tawny'.

Method: Add phase A into a disinfected heat resistant glass beaker and heat to 169°F/76°C to melt the waxes, stir. Add phase B (choose I or II) to phase A and stir until the color is uniform, then remove from heat. Add phase C, stir and pour while still liquid into eye shadow palette or small pots.

Phase A
Triglyceride 22.6% (6.8ml / 1 1/4tsp)

Polyisobutene-250 17% (5.1ml / 1tsp)

Beeswax 3% (0.9g / 1/2tsp)

Ozokerite 3% (0.9g / 1/4 - 1/2tsp)

Sorbitan Stearate 0.5% (0.15g / 1/16tsp)

Vitamin C L-Ascorbyl Palmitate 0.5% (0.15g / 1/16tsp)

Mica Spheres 9% (2.7g / 2tsp)

Mica Powder 11% (3.3g / 1Tbsp)

Bismuth Oxychloride 4% (1.2g / 1/2tsp)

Corn Starch AS 4% (1.2g / 1/2tsp)

Phase B
Mica Light Blue (I) or Mica Carmine Red (II) 8% (2.4g / 1 1/4tsp)

Mica Pearlwhite 14% (4.2g / 2 1/4tsp)

Mica Patina Silver Mica (I) or Mica Red (II) 2% (0.6g / 1/4tsp)

Phase C
Vitamin E Tocopherol 0.2% (0.1ml / 2 drops)

Phenoxyethanol-SA 1.2% (0.4ml / 10 drops)

Cream Shadow Stick (I)

Color: Violet, 50 g / 1.8 oz

Go Violet! This silky shadow has a creamy texture allowing easy application on the lid and providing a soft velvety finish. It is long-wearing and water-resistant. Can be poured into a lip balm tube or into pots. Can be applied with fingers or a cream eye shadow brush. Moving eyelid with a touch of violet looks stunning!

Method: Add phase A into a disinfected heat resistant glass beaker and heat to 169°F/76°C to melt the waxes, stir. Add phase B to phase A and stir until the color is uniform, then remove from the heat. Add phase C, stir and pour while still hot into lip balm tubes, shadow palette, or small pots

Phase A
Pearlwhite Mica 20% (10g / 1 1/2Tbsp)

Polyisobutene-250 29.3% (14.7ml / 1Tbsp)

Mica Powder 6% (3g / 1Tbsp)

Mica Spheres 6% (3g / 3/4Tbsp)

Corn Starch AS 4% (2g / 1/2tsp)

Beeswax 4.5% (2.3g / 1 1/4tsp)

Microcristalline Wax 7% (3.5g / 1/2Tbsp)

Ozokerite Wax 3% (1.5g / 1/2tsp)

Triglyceride 13% (6.5ml / 1 1/4tsp)

Phase B
Mica Blackstar Red 2% (1g / 1/2tsp)

Mica Bordeaux 2% (1g / 1/2tsp)

Mica Magenta 2% (1g / 1/2tsp)

Phase C
Vitamin E Tocopherol 0.2% (0.1ml / 2 drops)

Phenoxyethanol-SA 1% (0.5ml / 12 drops)

Cream Shadow Stick (II)

Color: Moss, 50 g / 1.8 oz

Wear green with patina silver and majestic green! Basically the same base recipe as recipe on page 148 but with different colors. Can be poured into a lip balm tube or into pots. Can be applied with fingers or cream eye shadow brush. Added as a finishing touch to the moving eye lid will look best!

Method: Add phase A into a disinfected heat resistant glass beaker and heat to 169°F/ 76°C to melt the waxes, stir. Add phase B to phase A and stir until the color is uniform, then remove from the heat. Add phase C, stir and pour while still hot into lip balm tubes, shadow palette, or small pots.

Phase A
Mica Pearlwhite 18% (9g / 1 1/2Tbsp)

Polyisobutene-250 29.3% (14.7ml / 1Tbsp)

Mica Powder 6% (3g / 1Tbsp)

Mica Spheres 6% (3g / 3/4Tbsp)

Corn Starch AS 4% (2g / 1/2tsp)

Beeswax 4.5% (2.3g / 1 1/4tsp)

Microcristalline Wax 7% (3.5g / 1/2Tbsp)

Ozokerite Wax 3% (1.5g / 1/2tsp)

Triglyceride 13% (6.5ml / 1 1/4tsp)

Phase B
Mica Majestic Green 6% (3g / 1 1/2tsp)

Mica Patina Silver 2% (1g / 1/2tsp)

Phase C
Vitamin E Tocopherol 0.2% (0.1ml / 2 drops)

Phenoxyethanol-SA 1% (0.5ml / 12 drops)

Mascara, Eyeliners & Eye Brow Shapers

Introduction

Mascara and eyeliners are some of the most popular beauty items. Mascara defines and brings color to the lashes, highlights and dramatizes eyes, and makes the lashes look thicker and longer. Ideally, coverage should be good, but the mascara should not clump on the lashes, flake during wear, or feel brittle after drying. Mascara can be tear-resistant, waterproof or water-resistant. Typical colors are black, brown, blue, and green, but you are open to create various different shades.

Liquid eyeliners and gel eyeliners have become increasingly popular since they are considered to be easier to apply, especially when the user wishes to shape and define the eyes with only a discreet and soft line. Eyeliner pencils (see page 122) are ideal for applying thicker, more dramatic strokes.

Formulation

Mascara: Mascara basically consists of a blend of waxes, pigments, texturizers, emulsifiers, and solvents.

The choice and amount of waxes determines, to a large part, the final characteristics of the formula such as thickness, consistency, and waterproof-ness. The most frequently used waxes are beeswax, carnauba wax, ozokerite wax, and microcrystalline wax.

Texturizers are important to provide body and to the mascara. Typical texturizers are corn starch, talc, magnesium stearate, micas, and bismuth oxychloride. Solvents used for mascara include glycerin, sorbitol, and volatile hydrocarbons such as isododecane, isoe-

icosane or polyisobutene. Volatile solvents have the advantage that part of the liquid in the mascara evaporates after application, making the mascara dry quicker.

Liquid Eyeliner & Gel Eyeliner: Liquid eyeliners are typically made as emulsion consisting of water, texturizers, pigments, emollients, and emulsifiers. Oftentimes polymers (e.g. carbomers or acrylate polymers like Gel-Maker EMU) are also incorporated. Polymers are useful in that they increase the viscosity and texture of the formula and also increase the adhesiveness of the eyeliner based on their film forming properties.

As outlined already on page 30, not all pigments are suitable for eye makeup products such as mascara and eyeliners. A number of organic dyes are not permitted for use in the eye area. Inorganic colors such as iron oxides, ultramarines and micas, however, are unproblematic for both mascara and liquid eyeliners.

Everyday Mascara (I)

Color: Dark Brown, 50 ml / 1.7 floz

Everyday essential for lashes. Formulated with provitamin B5 to define, condition and strengthen lashes. The formula is a smooth viscous fluid in dark brown color that won't flake. Water-resistant.

Method: Add phase C into a mortar and blend with the pestle until the color is uniform. Add phase A into disinfected heat resistant glass beaker. Add phase B into another glass beaker, sprinkle the gum arabic and the xanthan gum into the water while mixing to avoid the formation of lumps. Heat both beakers (phase A and B) to 185°F/85°C to melt the ingredients., stir. Add phase A to phase B and stir well with the hand mixer. Add phase C (from the mortar) to phase A/B while stirring and keep stirring for a few minutes until the color becomes uniform, keep the temperature at 167°F/75°C. When smooth and uniform add phase D, stir well, remove from heat. If too much water has evaporated and the mascara is pasty and thick, add a little more water and stir well. Fill while still hot into mascara containers using a syringe.

Phase A
Stearic Acid 5% (2.5g / 1tsp)
Beeswax 4.5% (2.3g / 1tsp)
Candelilla Wax 1.5% (0.8g / 1/4tsp)
Carnauba Wax 2.7% (1.4g / 1/2tsp)
Ceteareth-20 1.7% (0.9g / 1/4tsp)
Polyisobutene-800 1% (0.5ml / 1/4tsp)

Phase B
Distilled Water 64.1% (32ml / 2Tbsp + 1/2tsp)
Glycerin 2% (1ml / 1/4tsp)
Gum Arabic 1% (0.5g / 1/4tsp)
Xanthan Gum 0.5% (0.25g / 1/8tsp)

Phase C
Iron Oxide Brown 6% (3g / 3/4tsp)
Iron Oxide Black 5% (2.5g / 3/4tsp)
Mica Powder 3% (1.5g / 1/2Tbsp)

Phase D
Provitamin B5 0.8% (0.4ml / 10 drops)
Phenoxyethanol-SA 1.2% (0.6ml / 14 drops)

Everyday Mascara (II)
Color: Black, 50 ml / 1.7 floz

Similar recipe as on page 152 but with black color. Also formulated with provitamin B5 to define, condition and strengthen lashes. The mascara will be a smooth viscous fluid in black color that won't flake. Water-resistant.

Method: Add phase A into disinfected heat resistant glass beaker. Add phase B into another glass beaker, sprinkle the gum arabic and the xanthan gum into the water while mixing to avoid the formation of lumps. Heat both beakers (phase A and B) to 185°F/85°C to melt the ingredients, stir. Add phase A to phase B and stir well with the hand mixer. Add phase C to phase A/B while stirring and keep stirring for a few minutes until the color becomes uniform, keep the temperature at 167°F/75°C. When smooth and uniform add phase D, stir well, and remove from heat. If too much water has evaporated and the mascara is pasty and thick, add a little more water and stir well. Fill while still hot into mascara containers using a syringe.

Phase A
Stearic Acid 5% (2.5g / 1tsp)

Beeswax 4.5% (2.25g / 1tsp)

Candelilla Wax 1.5% (0.8g / 1/4tsp)

Carnauba Wax 2.7% (1.4g / 1/2tsp)

Ceteareth-20 1.7% (0.9g / 1/4tsp)

Polyisobutene-800 1% (0.5ml / 1/4tsp)

Phase B
Distilled Water 65.4% (32.7ml / 2Tbsp + 1/2tsp)

Glycerin 2% (1ml / 1/4tsp)

Gum Arabic 1% (0.5g / 1/4tsp)

Xanthan Gum 0.5% (0.3g / 1/8tsp)

Phase C
Iron Oxide Black 10% (5g / 1 3/4tsp)

Mica Powder 3% (1.5g / 1/2Tbsp)

Phase D
Provitamin B5 0.5% (0.25ml / 6 drops)

Phenoxyethanol-SA 1.2% (0.6ml / 14 drops)

Liquid Eyeliner
Color: Black, 50 ml / 1.7 floz

Liquid eyeliner that provides precise application. Formulated with black iron oxide for uniform black color. You may also use dark brown iron oxide for a brown color. Apply to dry-powdered lids and let dry.

Method: Add phase A into a mortar and mix well with the pestle until the color is uniform. Add phase B into a disinfected heat resistant glass beaker. Add phase C into another heat resistant glass beaker. Heat both beakers (phase B and phase C) to 150°F/65°C until ingredients are melted. Add phase A to phase C and stir well. Then add phase A/C to B and mix well. Remove from heat. Add phase D to phase A/B/C and stir again well. Fill the eyeliner into containers using a pipette.

Phase A
Iron Oxide Black 11% (5.5g / 1 3/4tsp)

Mica Spheres 10% (5g / 1Tbsp + 1/2tsp)

Phase B
Triglyceride 7% (3.5ml / 3/4tsp)

Stearic Acid 1.5% (0.75g / 1/4tsp)

Phase C
Distilled Water 64% (32ml / 2Tbsp + 1/2tsp)

Sulfosuccinate 0.3% (0.15ml / 3 drops)

Propylene Glycol 4% (2ml / 1/2tsp)

Phase D
GelMaker EMU 1% (0.5ml / 12 drops)

Phenoxyethanol/SA 1.2% (0.6ml / 14 drops)

Gel Eyeliner
Color: Black, 50 ml / 1.7 floz

This black eyeliner offers the precision of liquid liners and the ease of a gel-based formula. The color is long-wearing and water-resistant. Apply to dry-powdered lids and let dry.

Method: Add phase A into a disinfected glass beaker and stir to mix the ingredients. Add phase B to another glass beaker. Heat both beakers to 167°F/75°C until the wax is melted. Add phase A slowly to phase B and stir very well with the hand mixer, to form the gel and to mix the two phases. Remove from the heat and add phase C, stir well. Adjust viscosity with GelMaker EMU, or if too thick dilute with water. Fill into pot containers.

Phase A
Distilled Water 65.5% (32.8g / 2Tbsp + 1tsp)

Sulfosuccinate 0.3% (0.15ml / 3 drops)

Iron Oxide Black 11% (5.5g / 1 3/4tsp)

Mica Powder 5% (2.5g / 3/4Tbsp)

Phase B
Triglyceride 7% (3.5ml / 3/4tsp)

Candelilla Wax 5% (2.5g / 1tsp)

GelMaker EMU 3% (1.5ml / 36 drops)

Microcrystalline Wax 2% (1g / 1/2tsp)

Phase C
Phenoxyethanol-SA 1.2% (0.6ml / 14 (

Pressed Powder Eyeliner
Color: Dark Espresso, 30 g / 1.0 oz

Eyeliner in powder form that is pressed and applied with a dampened eyeliner brush. Can also be used as a brow filler.

Method: Add phase B into a mortar and blend well until uniform. Add phase A to the mortar as well and blend with the pestle until uniform. The powder may clump to the pestle at the beginning, just scratch it off with a clean spatula add it back to the powder and blend until the powder and emollients are well mixed. Add phase C to the mortar and blend again until uniform. Press into pots or pans.

Phase A
Polyisobutene-250 10.5% (3.1ml / 1/2tsp)
Meadowfoam Seed Oil 4% (1.2ml / 1/4tsp)
Polyglyceryl Oleate 2% (0.6ml / 14 drops)
Vitamin E Tocopherol 0.5% (0.15ml / 5 drops)

Phase B
Iron Oxide Black 15% (4.5g / 1 1/2tsp)
Iron Oxide Brown 7% (2.1g / 1/2tsp)
Corn Starch AS 10% (3g / 1tsp)
Magnesium Stearate 4% (1.2g / 1/2tsp)

Phase C
Mica Powder 46% (13.8g / 4Tbsp + 1tsp)
Phenoxyethanol-SA 1% (0.3ml / 7 drops)

Eye Brow Shaper
Color: Medium Brown, 30 ml / 1.0 floz

Cream-gel formula for a medium brown brow shaper that effortlessly defines and fills in brows while controlling and shaping them. Formulated with provitamin B5 to condition and nourish.

Method: Add phase A into a mortar and blend the pigments with the pestle. Add phase B into glass beaker. Add phase A to phase B and stir. Combine phase C, stir and add to phase A/B, blend well with a little hand mixer to form the gel. Adjust viscosity with Gel-Maker EMU, stir for a few minutes to make sure the color is uniform. Add phase D to phase A/B/C and stir again well. Fill the brow shaper into a mascara tube using a syringe.

Phase A
Iron Oxide Brown 1% (0.3g / 1/8tsp)

Iron Oxide Black 0.3% (0.1g / 1/16tsp)

Phase B
Distilled Water 87.1% (26ml / 5 tsp)

Glycerin 2% (0.6ml / 14 drops)

Sulfosuccinate 0.3% (0.1ml / 2 drops)

Phase C
GelMaker EMU 2% (0.6ml / 14 drops)

Triglyceride 6% (1.8ml / 1/4 - 1/2tsp)

Phase D
Provitamin B5 0.5% (0.15ml / 4 drops)

Paraben-DU 0.8% (0.24ml / 3 drops)

The Perfect Makeup

Tips for Applying Makeup

Makeup can boost your confidence and overall feel-good factor. For a great make-over you must start with the right foundation. Whereas eye shadow, lipstick, and blusher accent the face, it is the foundation that sets the tone for a woman's appearance.

Foundation

▦ Test foundation along your jaw line - not on your hand or wrist. View it under different light settings. It must match the natural color of your neck. The foundation shade that is right is one that disappears into the skin. Those with darker skin tones and yellow undertones must avoid foundations with a pink underbase. This could make the skin look grey.

▦ Make sure your foundation is sheer and light to prevent caking. Apply it on a clean and moisturised face. If you want your foundation to look sheer, apply it with a sponge. For more coverage apply it with your fingertips or brush.

▦ Do not forget to blend foundation around hairline, ears, jaw line, upper neck, eyelids and lips. Open your mouth when applying foundation to expose the neck area and eliminate an obvious line at the jaw line.

▦ To give the skin a dewy finish, moisten a gauze pad or wash cloth in astringent and gently pat your already made up face. The astringent (e.g. witch hazel) removes the matte look of the makeup, while leaving the skin radiant.

▦ Thick foundation can be mixed with some light moisturiser to give a sheer finish.

Face Powder

▦ Powdering after foundation helps set the foundation, absorbs oil and serves as a boost for a flawless look.

▦ Use loose powder to set makeup and compact powder for easy touch-ups during the day or night.

▦ Apply powders with a large powder brush or a powder puff. For acneic skin use a disposable cotton pad instead of a brush. This will avoid transferring bacteria into the powder container and back to your skin.

▦ Keep your compact face powder handy for touch ups during the day.

Concealer

▦ A concealer should match your skin tone or be one shade lighter. Use it to cover dark circles around the eyes, and any discoloration on the face. Apply concealer under foundation so it will cover and not be rubbed off.

▦ Use a green-based concealer (add a small amount of chromium oxide green to the recipe) if you think you over-blush above acceptable levels. It also hides pimples, blemishes, scars, birthmarks and broken capillaries. Use a yellow concealer to cover up dark colored under-eye circles.

▦ Concealer should be applied as sparingly as possible. Apply it gently in a dabbing motion. Do not rub or exert pressure.

Mineral Makeup

▥ Use mineral makeup after applying a moisturizer that has been completely absorbed.

▥ Apply mineral makeup in thin layers with a large powder brush or Kabuki brush until the desired coverage is reached. The more mineral makeup you apply the more coverage you will get. Use a high-quality brush.

Blush

▥ Use two different blush shades: a natural shade and a second coat of a brighter, more colorful blush. This gives a more natural look and more depth.

▥ Use blush sparingly and spread it on the apple of the cheek (fleshy, lifted part of the cheek when you smile in an exaggerated way). If you have very high cheekbones apply blush on the center of the face. If you have a full face, apply blush more to your hairline.

▥ Use a full brush to apply blush. Discard the brushes that come with blush compacts; they are too small.

▥ Never overdo your blush application, tap excess blush off your brush before applying. To tone down blush, apply a dusting of powder on top to subdue the color. In the evening you can go a bit heavier.

Lipstick & Lip Gloss

▥ Try mixing different shades of lipstick. You might discover a unqiue color. Start with a light color first and add a darker on top.

▥ For an even look cover also the corners of your mouth. Using a lip brush will cover the lip better and the color will stay longer.

▥ To create your own smudge-resistant lipstick blot your lips with one sheet of twoply tissue. Re-apply lipstick and blot again. This will absorb the oils in the product and leave the pigment and matte waxes.

▥ Massage lips with your toothbrush. This promotes blood circulation and makes your lips smooth and less chapped.

▥ Lip gloss can be used alone or over lipstick colors for an extra shine.

Lip Liner

▥ Use a lip liner pencil with the same shade as your lipstick or a little lighter. Never wear lip liner and lipstick colors together when they are contrasting colors. When wearing a red lipstick, use a brown lip liner all over first as the red pigment will last longer.

▥ Apply lip liner to the outline and fill in your lips. Follow then with a gloss or lipstick.

Eye Shadow

▥ When applying eye shadow to the crease of the eye, keep your eyes open and slightly tilt your head backward. This will enable you to better see the shape. Apply the eyeshadow along the lash line. This creates a soft line.

▥ Avoid applying moisturizer or foundation onto your eyelids as this will crease the eye shadow.

▥ If you have puffy eyelids do not use iridescent or frosted shadows in light colors or white. Use softer, matte colors. For more mature skin use iridescent shades sparingly.

▥ If your eye shadow looks too strong do not rub it off. Just dust face powder over it.

Eyeliner

When using an eye pencil, open your mouth slightly to relax the eye muscles. It will make lining a lot easier without having to pull or tug at your lid.

Do not apply eyeliner at the inside rim of your eye. This may increase the risk of injuring the eye.

Apply eyeliner as close as possible and even into the lashes to avoid the white line you sometimes get when liner and lashes do not connect.

Mascara

Apply mascara to the upper lashes from underneath. Applying mascara onto the top will look heavy. Always use less mascara on your lower lashes.

Apply a few coats and wait between coats until the mascara has been dried. If it is too wet use a tissue to remove excess color.

Blot the mascara brush on a tissue to remove excess color. You can use it then for coloring your eye brows.

Eye Brow Liner

Always use a brow color that is as natural looking as possible. The main objective is to define, not create over-powering brows. To fill in, comb first, then use feather like strokes with your pencil to fill in.

When using powdered brow color, use a harder bristled angle brow brush and draw tiny hair-like strokes. When using a brow pencil, maintain a sharp edge and use the same technique as the brush.

Index

Notes

Notes

Notes

Notes